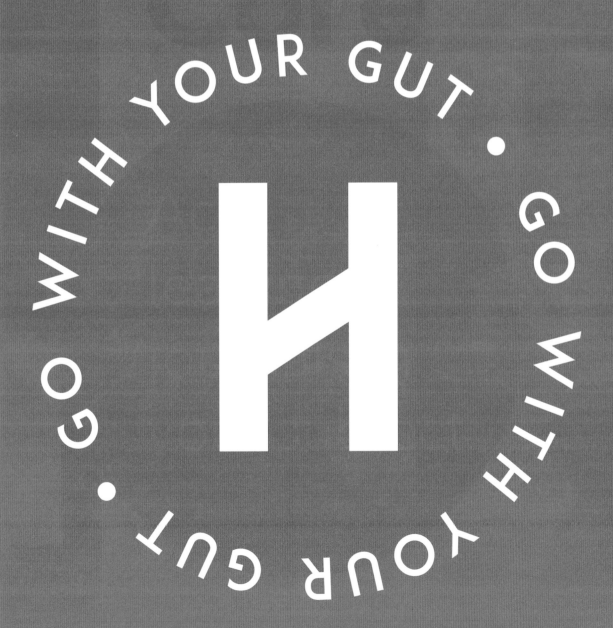

GO WITH YOUR GUT • GO WITH YOUR GUT • GO WITH YOUR GUT • GO WITH YOUR GUT •

CONTENTS

NATURAL, FERMENTED, LIVING FOOD

HIGH
MOOD FOOD

*Our story, Our recipes,
Our way of life*

HOW DO YOU LIVE A MORE FULFILLED AND SATISFYING LIFE?

WELCOME BY
URSEL BARNES

When I worked as an executive coach, the focus was on performance and better communication. My successful and talented clients travelled extensively and worked irregular and long hours. Their work/life balance always seemed to be a tricky issue. 'Me time' - favouring regular sleep, nutritious food and a sunny disposition - seemed to fall victim to the multiple demands of work and family. Everyday energy drains like commuting and travelling made it nearly impossible to fit in time for physical and mental health.

A healthy spirit thrives in a healthy body. It is difficult to find a nutrient-dense lunch in a 30 minute break, and to eat a healthy dinner at a reasonable time when you are working and living a busy life.

I have practiced Qi Gong since my early twenties, and am inspired by my grandmaster's advice:

Food is the best medicine
You are your own best doctor
Time is the best treatment

   NATURAL · FERMENTED · LIVING FOOD

For centuries people have eaten plants, herbs and berries for optimal nutrition and used their healing properties to treat diseases. We are part of nature but seem to have lost our way when the food processing industry created highly addictive and nutritionally void food. Allergies and mental health issues have increased sharply.

The gut and brain work together. A calm attitude and having physical energy and resilience are the result of their joint effort to keep the body well balanced. Science is now able to prove what common wisdom has known all along: food can and should be considered medicine. Do you agree that you could be your own best doctor? It's likely that nobody has actually fed you since you were able to hold your own spoon as a toddler. It is your choice what you put in your mouth. We need to be more aware of how we feel after we eat. Do we hit energy lows after certain meals? Do we get bloated or do we suffer from cravings? Those feelings are often directly linked to what we have eaten a couple of hours before. We don't need to detox our bodies: we need to detox our minds from unhealthy habits. Don't focus on what you do wrong. Simply include healthier food choices into your way of life and you might just push out the things that are not good for you.

Whether you suffer from a broken heart or a nasty bout of flu, grandmother was probably right when she advised that time is the best healer and you would do well to stay in bed and rest. At our High Mood Food cafés, we prepare food with time for people who don't have time. We ferment, soak, activate and sprout to offer the best nutrients in their most absorbable form, presented in delicious dishes. Our clients lead busy lifestyles but appreciate real food made by people who care. Time is of the essence.

In these new times living with the coronavirus, we are spending more time at home and I would like to encourage you to try our recipes and make your own ferments. It's fun to have different cultures bubbling away in your kitchen and getting to know their 'personalities'. Find your own best way of eating and understand what makes you feel satiated and content. It's all in the name: if you eat well, your gut will grant you resilience, improved immunity, better cognitive function and put a smile on your face!

In this book, we will talk about the significance of real food for a healthy gut. We'll also take you on a journey into fermenting and show you how easy it is to make and keep some staple ferments in your fridge, just as our ancestors would have done to preserve their food throughout the seasons. You might need a few helpings to get used to the tangy and sour flavours. The tastes can be acquired! Start slowly with small portions. Once your gut bacteria meet their pre- and probiotic friends, they will most likely signal your brain that you want more, and put you in high spirits!

Guten Appetit!

≋ ⚡ ☙ ♡ ◉ NATURAL · FERMENTED · LIVING FOOD

HOW TO USE THIS BOOK

We have brought together recipes for the drinks and dishes that we serve at our cafés.

Our first meal of the day is called **'break ya fast'** as it will end your fast from the evening before, which can be eaten either earlier or later in the day (see page 64).

Lunch and dinner are built around different tasty and nutritional options including soups, salads and your protein of choice: chicken, fish or tempeh (see page 113).

Our afternoon **snacks** can be enjoyed as a treat at any time of the day (see page 187) .

We have also included a section on **seasonal spreads** (see page 217) and **party food** for entertaining at home (see page 295).

Last but not least, there is a chapter on **Kids and the 5 K** (see page 287) because you can never start too early!

We encourage you to try something new, adapt recipes and swap ingredients to suit your personal needs. Enjoy, have fun and **go with your gut!**

HIGH'S FAVOURITE STAPLE INGREDIENTS

- Your homemade 5 K ferments
- Seasonal fresh veg and fruit
- Soaked and activated nuts and seeds
- Tempeh
- Local and happy animal protein (meat, fish, eggs)
- Other ferments (miso, soy sauce)
- Herbs, spices (e.g. turmeric, pepper, chilli)
- Salt (Himalayan or Maldon)

- Healthy fats (extra virgin olive oil, extra virgin coconut oil, ghee)
- Pulses (lentils, chickpeas, beans)
- Gluten-free flour (buckwheat, almond, coconut)
- Grains (brown rice, quinoa, millet)
- Ancient grain flour (Khorasan wheat, spelt)
- Good quality dark chocolate
- Honey, maple syrup, coconut sugar
- Stevia

WHAT DOES IT MEAN
TO BE HEALTHY?

We are healthy when we feel energetic, sleep well and have a positive outlook on life. Physical and mental health relies on a well-functioning gut that is able to absorb nutrients from our food. We have trillions of gut bacteria in our digestive tract and our brains are constantly fed messages from these little soldiers. Our mental health relies on positive messages from our gut. If we eat good nutrients, the bacteria that give us positive feedback will thrive and if we eat badly, our mood levels might suffer.

Simply put, there are three categories of food groups:

GREENS AND VEGETABLES
We all agree that we should eat more of these

These are our main source of vitamins, nutrients, trace elements and insoluble fibre: the prebiotics.

ARTIFICIAL ADDITIVES,
WHITE SUGAR AND TRANS FATS
We should try to avoid these

These can be considered to be nutritionally unhelpful. White sugar usually results in quick absorption into the bloodstream and causes blood sugar spikes. Additives and trans fats are shown to cause adverse health risks through high heat and artificial processing.

PROTEINS

These offer important nutritional building blocks which everybody needs and can be found in meat, fish, eggs and pulses, which are not in themselves good or bad. Individual taste, ethical choices and performance goals will determine the sources of protein we choose.

For High Mood Food, we decided to make vegetables and greens the main element of the dish and to add a protein of choice as the side dish. We support a flexitarian, individual and pro-choice approach to food as lifestyle medicine.

We avoid all nasties and use local, seasonal and nutrient-dense ingredients wherever possible.

Beyond food, it is super important to eat mindfully. The journey of our food begins with our eyes and meanders through our mouth and stomach, long before it reaches the gut. We digest better if we take the time to enjoy, and chew, allowing the food to travel through its many signposts. It is a slow-jog marathon that should be honoured with attention and care, and not be treated as a sprint. Energy flows where attention goes. If your eyes are focused on a screen, you are sending your energy to the viedo you're watching or the recipient of your email. The energy is not going to your stomach and digestive tract. Take a pause, sit down and avoid confrontation or arguments while eating.

A healthy salad eaten in a rush is probably not as digestible as a fast food hamburger eaten with delight and gusto.

HOW DID WE GET HERE?

At High Mood Food we support our clients to choose real food.

We aim to source our ingredients locally because we serve our gut bacteria best with food that has evolved and grown in our own geographic habitat. Short transport times after harvesting offer the best density of nutrients, as food loses nutritional value during long periods between picking and consumption. Whenever possible, consider the quality of the soil where the ingredients are grown.

A variety of fresh vegetables ensures that our intake of prebiotics will nourish our healthy gut bacteria. Vegetables and whole plant-based foods are rich in fibre which is the main source of prebiotics. Insoluble fibre, like flax seeds or psyllium husk, passes the digestive tract and is not acted on or fermented in the colon. It provides no nutrition to the bacteria but holds a lot of water and helps to maintain softer, more regular bowel movements. Soluble fibre is used by the colon's bacteria as a food source. Healthy gut bacteria help to strengthen the bowel wall, improve the body's ability to absorb essential nutrients and have been shown to produce hormones that control appetite and anxiety, and improve cognitive function and resilience.

An ideal ratio of prebiotics to probiotics is about 70:30. Probiotics are live micro-organisms which can help to support a healthy microbiome. Fermented foods offer the benefits of probiotics which support our own healthy gut bacteria and can help to fight pathogens in the gut. The good bacteria grow during the fermentation process. Some people don't like the taste of fermented foods or feel it is easier to take a probiotic supplement. It is unfortunately not always certain that the live micro-organisms can survive the acidity of the stomach and reach the digestive tract alive. Fermented foods have offered the benefits of a wide range of natural probiotics for many centuries, if not thousands of years.

SEASONAL

FERMENTED

Probiotics

Local

VEGCENTRIC

BEYOND FOOD

Prebiotics

Individual
Intuitive
Mindful

Happy *Gut*

GUT

HIGHLY NOURISHING

ENERGY

HIGHLY ENERGISING

CALM

HIGHLY

RELAXING

IMMUNE

HIGHLY STRENGTHENING

BRAIN

HIGHLY FOCUSING

     NATURAL · FERMENTED · LIVING FOOD

HIGH MOOD FOOD'S RECIPES
ARE FREE FROM...

...modern wheat and toxins.
They are also low in sugar.

Some things are good for everybody and general health is part of High's vision. Sugar, wheat and some ingredients in highly processed foods have been shown to cause deteriorating physical and mental health.

High's recipes are free from processed sugars and even low in natural sugars. Our taste buds and gut bacteria adapt quite quickly; if you have a sweet tooth, why not try using less sugar for a while and substitute it with less harmful sweeteners? You might be surprised how sweet a piece of fruit can taste once you have weaned yourself off sugary sweets. We don't have to detox our bodies, we have to detox our minds to remove destructive habits and toxic cravings before we can go with our gut, and trust our gut feeling that what we want to eat is in fact good for us.

Wheat has been shown to cause harm to the gut lining and has been linked to various illnesses such as allergies and leaky gut syndrome. Even if you are not tested to be gluten intolerant, we would suggest to generally stay wheat-free. Other gluten containing grains like rye and barley, or an ancient wheat grain like Kamut, are fine when properly fermented, sprouted or soaked.

Get into the habit of reading the label and stay away from terms such as dextrose, maltose, trans fats, and hydrogenated oil. Canned, frozen or cooked food items loaded up with these ingredients can hide almost twice the daily recommended amount of sodium and sugar. Many thickeners are just used to make liquids more appealing, rather than splitting, and some harmful oils just make biscuits crunchier. Get used to wonky fruit, denser textures, and give your drink a little shake to mix up the content. The taste will be more authentic, and your tummy will thank you.

   NATURAL · FERMENTED · LIVING FOOD

FLEXITARIAN AND VEG-CENTRIC

Once we have ensured that our food stays away from harmful substances, High Mood Food endorses a flexitarian lifestyle that caters for individual tastes, lifestyles and training goals. Whether you choose to be vegetarian, vegan, paleo, high-protein, grain-free, dairy-free, low-carb, gluten-free or high-fat, the High way of eating will offer you plenty of choice for a wholesome intake of yummy nutrients. We are not part of a weight-loss movement. Some people are luckier with their gut bacteria and will be able to metabolise calories more quickly. If you want to lose a few pounds, introduce some new habits into your lifestyle. Eat your carbs earlier in the day and give your digestion a rest in the evenings and overnight, eat one or two spoonfuls of psyllium husk - a great prebiotic that will fill you up and help to make your bowel movements regular - or simply skip the escalators and say yes to the stairs wherever you can.

Go with YOUR gut. Try new ingredients and aim to have as many different plants as possible every week. Find out if there is a foresting activity where you live or, if you are rooted in the city, why not visit a friend or relative who lives in the country and enjoy some wholesome forest-bathing with them?

You might think that 'veg-centric' is just a buzzword, but we are excited about new ways of preparing old-fashioned veg. Have you tried turmeric-roasted cauliflower steaks with their crispy leaves? Or used some dehydrated kimchi salt as seasoning? We love chargrilled baby gem salads, and romaine lettuce grilled in the oven then dipped in any of our probiotic dressings: simple pleasures and new taste profiles. Many vegetables taste very different depending on their method of preparation. Onion is an excellent prebiotic; the taste is astringent and crunchy when uncooked, but sweet and soft when sautéed in butter or baked in the oven. Cauliflower is a plain carb-free alternative to rice, but has a distinct flavour when cooked in a soup and this changes again when charred or simply oven-baked.

Most nutrients will suffer from high heat or frying. Try to use gentle methods of preparation when possible and keep high heat for flavour combinations and special treats. Use the whole vegetable in its skin to protect the nutrients. We think oven-roasted leaves are a toasty treat: try kale chips, broccoli stems or cavolo nero sprinkled with olive oil and sea salt.

FOOD MADE WITH TIME
Soaking, germinating, sprouting, activating

Soaking, sprouting and activating are traditional preparation methods which alter the nutritional profile of nuts, seeds, legumes and grains to make them more digestible for humans. For soaking, the ingredient is covered with water and allowed to sit for varying lengths of time. Doing this before cooking the ingredient reduces the level of toxins and antinutrients, such as enzyme inhibitors and lectins which can cause digestive troubles such as bloating or diarrhoea. Phytic acid inhibits the absorption of some nutrients in these foods and the positive enzyme activity of trypsin. It is at least partially broken down during the soaking process.

A good rule of thumb is to soak grains and pulses overnight (12 hours or even up to 24 hours) in clean water. Drain and rinse until the water runs clear. To further increase digestibility and nutritional value, you may choose to germinate your seeds or grains. Germination is a preliminary step to sprouting, increasing the level of vitamins and enhancing digestibility even further. To do this, let the seeds or grains rest for a couple of days after soaking, rinsing them every now and then to keep them moist.

Fully sprouting your grains and letting them grow into little plants will lead to higher vitamin levels, but please bear in mind that the sprouted raw grain still has higher phytic acid levels than the cooked produce and should therefore only be eaten in moderation. Soaking nuts in salt water is the most effective way to reduce the antinutrient content. Just like grains and pulses, soak them overnight or leave for up to 24 hours. The harder the nut, the longer the soak. Seeds such as pumpkin and sunflower, as well as softer nuts such as walnuts and macadamias, prefer shorter soaking times of up to 6 hours. Use a dehydrator, the oven (at a maximum of 50°c) or let them dry in the sunshine until truly dehydrated to avoid mould.

Activating is the process of soaking and dehydrating ingredients to enhance their nutritional profile and digestibility. At High Mood Food we soak, sprout or activate all our nuts, seeds, legumes and grains so we would advise the same for home usage. Chia and flax seeds contain high amounts of soluble fibres. Chia seeds can absorb up to 12 times their weight in water. Cracking chia and flax seeds enable higher nutrient absorption and letting the seeds swell prevents constipation. We recommend cracking chia seeds in a mortar or blitzing them for a few seconds in a blender, then letting the liquid be absorbed for 20 to 30 minutes before consumption.

   NATURAL • FERMENTED • LIVING FOOD

GO
WITH
YOUR
GUT

NATURAL · FERMENTED · LIVING FOOD

THE GUT-BRAIN CONNECTION

What we eat and our mood go hand in hand. Our brain and gut actually develop from the same cluster of embryonic tissue and remain closely connected.

We know that the neurotransmitter serotonin might be produced in the brain but is mostly stored in the gastro-intestinal tract. This naturally implies that taking care of our gut will influence our mood, how we feel and probably even our outlook on life! 'I have a gut feeling' and 'go with your gut!' or 'I have butterflies in my tummy' are expressions that show how the gut-brain connection has been viscerally experienced for many centuries.

We eat to nourish our bodies, to nourish ourselves. There are very old traditions of food preparation that were developed by our ancestors. Fermentation is an ancient technique: archaeological findings suggest that intentional fermentation has been a common practice for close to 10,000 years.

The gastrointestinal (GI) tract is the biggest organ in the human body.

The enteric nervous system is actually two thin layers of more than 100 million nerve cells lining the gastrointestinal tract that are in constant communication with the brain. There is emerging research that digestive system activity may affect cognitive skills. By supporting the internal ecosystem, the microbiome and by eating pre- and probiotics, we indirectly support brain function. Research indicates that traditional dietary practices and positive mental health may be linked.

The human brain is nearly 60% fat and so it seems wise to provide the body with the best building blocks by eating healthy fats such as cold-pressed oils and the omega 3 fats contained in nuts and seeds or wild salmon and other fatty fish.

However, the food we eat is not just the total sum of micro- and macronutrients; it takes care of our bodies and minds on many levels. Forgetting all the science, we have seen many clients leaving our café going about their day with a smile on their face; simply knowing that you are eating delicious and healthy meals may boost your mood!

MOOD FOOD
FRESHLY MADE
EVERY DAY
ALL DAY

  NATURAL • FERMENTED • LIVING FOOD

A MESSAGE FROM THE HIGH TEAM

We loved working at London's first gut health café. All of us came from different backgrounds with different reasons for being there, but we all shared a passion for health, nutrition and helping people. Working at High didn't feel like work (apart from the crazy lunch rush resulting in queues out of the door) but a place where every individual felt seen, respected and supported. As cheesy as it might sound, we became family. Most of us have always been passionate about health and eating well but didn't fully value our gut health as much as we should, priding ourselves on 'going with our gut' for decisions and choices in life, but not always for what we were eating and drinking. Sometimes we felt too busy to eat, grabbing a quick snack or skipping meals completely.

Working at High showed us just how important it is to give your body what it needs. The gut is the second brain of the body and if your gut is happy and healthy, you will be happy and healthy. Through taking time in the day to sit and fully appreciate your food while eating mindfully we all noticed such a difference in our mood, overall health and energy levels. Everything in our café was made fresh in our kitchen downstairs. From creating menus and recipes to cooking and serving customers, all our tasks were done with so much passion and love. Each salad has a different active, living or fermented element that took a long time to ferment to perfection. The krauts, kimchis and dressings are all handmade in small batches, patiently left to soak, sprout, ferment or activate to serve the tastiest and most nutritionally dense food we could. It really is slow food that you can eat fast… but not too fast!

The best thing about our work was meeting all the incredible people that came in for their morning coffee, lunch or daily almond butter cookie. Office workers, celebrities, yogis or retail workers; serving them was a joy. Some came in stressed, tired and 'hangry' but once they had taken time for themselves to sit down and eat or drink mindfully, while switching off from work, they would seem to leave a completely different person.

One thing we learnt was to have everything in moderation. Live a happy healthy life. Eat well and if you want a little bit of cake or a brownie, have it! But don't feel guilt or shame when you eat it. Just enjoy every mouthful. At High we always aim to be inclusive, because we understand that everyone is so different with their own unique gut bacteria, tastes and nutritional needs. And hopefully in this book we have catered to that.

There really is something for everyone with High Mood Food!

HAVE YOU HAD YOUR 5 K?

ANCIENT RECIPES FOR MODERN TIMES

We are slowly discovering what some of our great-grandmothers knew and practiced intuitively: different vegetables and fruit conserved in salt brine are really good for you!

Before we had fridges, many people in different cultures used fermentation to preserve vegetables for the long winter months. For example, Russians often grow up on kefir and kvas, Koreans eat kimchi as one of their staple foods, Germans love kraut with sausages, and the Japanese - who are known for having the oldest population in the world - eat miso and natto, which are forms of fermented soy high in vitamin K2, associated with supporting bone density and other health benefits.

FOSTERING HEALTHY BACTERIA

Traditional lacto-fermentation has been utilised by many cultures for centuries to preserve perishable goods, thus making fruits and vegetables available all year around. In fact, archaeological findings suggest that intentional fermentation has been in common practice for close to 10,000 years.

This practice had gone out of fashion when modern food processing became popular. Instead of lengthy fermentation processes, time-saving methods for preservation were introduced using vinegar, high heat processing, pasteurising, canning, and deep-freezing.

The downside of food processing became apparent with the alarming rise of allergies, intolerances and many kinds of gut-related health issues.

    NATURAL • FERMENTED • LIVING FOOD

In the last decade a new grassroots movement set out to change the way we view and connect to food. People were fed up with not finding cures for their various health issues. Some outside the box thinking led to a new look at fermentation, the rediscovery of ancient preparation techniques and the reintroduction of these methods to the mainstream. Personal stories of healing are frequent, and doctors are starting to promote the importance of gut health. Research is being done to prove what used to be common knowledge: good (beneficial) bacteria in the gut have preventative and healing properties.

Around 85% of the bacterial population in a healthy lower digestive tract is made up of beneficial bacteria. When the ratio between good and bad bacteria tips, the harmful bacteria take over and the imbalance in the microbiome impacts our health negatively. Dysbiosis, the name for microbial imbalance, can cause skin conditions, constipation and diarrhoea. It can also lead to weight gain and may be the root cause for various chronic health conditions.

Bacteria such as Lactobacillus acidophilus and Bifidobacterium lactis are the agents in the fermentation process that make probiotic-rich foods. Probiotics are good bacteria similar or even identical to the bacteria living inside our bodies. Consumption of fermented food therefore supports a healthy gut flora.

KEFIR

Kefir means 'foam and bubbles' and is a slightly sour yoghurt-like drink made from animal milk.

Traditional kefir was made in goatskin bags that were hung near a doorway and got knocked by anyone passing by to keep the grains and milk well mixed. Water kefir is a refreshing alternative that uses different cultures for the fermentation process.

DAIRY KEFIR

Kefir is made by fermenting milk with kefir grains, sometimes in the form of freeze-dried kefir starters. Kefir has a lovely thick consistency with a slightly sour taste.

Kefir grains contain yeasts, lactic acid and acetic acid bacteria. After inoculating the milk of your choice with kefir cultures, they will start to transform the milk by breaking down lactose into lactic acid, giving kefir its distinctive acidic flavour.

Whether you use cow's, goat's or sheep's milk, full-fat milk will yield the best results. If you don't want to use raw milk, you can use pasteurised milk but we recommend avoiding homogenised and other highly processed milk products. Lactose is the main allergen in milk and it is also the sugar that the bacteria feed on. As most of the lactose is converted into lactic acid by the kefir culture, many people who are sensitive to lactose can drink kefir.

Making your own dairy kefir is a simple process. All you need is a clean vessel for the milk and the kefir grains, such as a glass bottle or Kilner jar, and a sieve or a spoon. We recommend using a Kilner jar, which will allow any excess pressure to be released without contaminating your kefir.

It is easy to find 'kefir buddies' on the internet: other kefir aficionados will usually happily share their grains. Even if you have been producing your own kefir for a while, it may be interesting to try out different grains.

For a flavoured kefir, mix 150ml of kefir with 30g of fresh fruit (pure or compote). We recommend giving mango, berry or chai spice a go for your morning snack.

a. Kefir grains with fresh organic milk
b. Pouring the milk over the kefir grains
c. Storing the kefir grains to be kept in the fridge
(use cream if stored for longer than a week)
d. Your own homemade kefir!

HOW TO MAKE DAIRY KEFIR:

Fill a 1L Kilner jar with the milk of your choice. Add 1 tablespoon of kefir grains. With the lid on, leave the jar in a quiet place and let the kefir culture work for about 24 hours. Moving the jar around every now and then actually helps fermenting activity.

Strain the milk through a sieve to remove the grains. You could use a stainless steel spoon or clean hands instead. There is an urban legend that touching your kefir with metal will harm the grains, but this is definitely not the case if using stainless steel. If you do not want to make another batch straight away, put your grains in a small jar of cream and keep them in the fridge.

For optimal taste, try varying the length of fermentation at ambient temperatures or prolong the process by continuing the culturing process in the fridge for another day or two. Experimenting with the conditions of fermentation will yield different tastes.

If you are looking for a cultured alternative to sour cream or cream cheese, you can easily make your own. Longer fermentation time is the key. Once your kefir separates into whey and curds, strain off the liquid. After removing your kefir grains, put the curds into a cheesecloth sitting on a bowl and let the vessel rest for up to 24 hours in your fridge. Kefir cream cheese can be enjoyed savoury or sweet by adding herbs, garlic, vanilla or cinnamon.

If your kefir separates during the process, just use a whisk to incorporate the solids again for a creamy texture. You could also try a double or triple fermenting process: strain the whey and leave the grains in the kefir. When the kefir mix has rested in the fridge overnight, add fresh milk and let the mix ferment again at room temperature for another couple of hours. This process can be repeated a third time and will yield a very creamy kefir similar to a clotted cream.

NON-DAIRY KEFIR

Dairy kefir grains feed best on full-fat dairy milk. However, it is possible to use non-dairy milks such as oat, almond or coconut to make dairy-free and vegan kefir.

The grains will usually not feed well on non-dairy milks for multiple productions. If you want to keep your kefir grains alive and thriving, you need to give the little guys regular 'treatments' by soaking them in animal milk or cream!

YOGHURT

While yoghurt is not one of our 5 Ks, it is also a fermented drink in its own right. Making yoghurt is a different process from kefir altogether.

You start by heating milk just below boiling point to denature the proteins within it. After cooling the milk to about room temperature, inoculate the milk using your yoghurt of choice. The rule of thumb is to use 1 tablespoon of yoghurt for every litre (or 4 cups) of milk.

Combine a little yoghurt and milk then add this mixture back into the rest of the milk. Keep your container (or containers, if you like to pre-portion) at about 45 to 50°c for at least 12 hours and in the fridge thereafter.

You can vary the length of the fermentation time to play around with the taste profile. It is commonly assumed that after a fermentation time of 24 hours, no lactose is left for the bacteria to feed on.

〰 ⚡ ⚘ ♡ ◉ NATURAL • FERMENTED • LIVING FOOD

KEFIR CULTURED BUTTER

500g double cream
100g kefir grains
5g salt

Wrap the kefir grains in a muslin cloth and then add the grains to
the double cream. Ferment at an ambient temperature for 36 hours.
Remove the grains and chill the jar in the fridge until set.

Place the fermented double cream and salt in an electric mixer and whisk.
Initially the mixture will turn to whipped cream with stiff peaks but after a
while, it will break down and separate into butterfat and buttermilk. Pour
everything into a fresh piece of muslin cloth and set over a colander.
Allow the buttermilk to drain off and reserve it in the fridge for later use.

When most of the buttermilk has drained off, tightly squeeze the muslin
cloth to make sure all of the excess liquid has drained out. A good way
of checking this is to squeeze the muslin while submerged in a bowl of
ice-cold water. At first, the water will turn cloudy. Pour away the cloudy
water and repeat two or three times until the water stays clear.

Did you Know

Yes, you can eat butter and it's good for you! Cultured butter has live bacteria
and yeast added to the cream in the form of kefir grains. It is then left to culture
before churning into butter. The good fats will help you focus, the fatty acids
provide energy and the vitamins will keep your joints in good health.

KEFIR ICE CREAM

2 eggs
30g maple syrup
300ml kefir (see page 28)
150ml double cream
1 tsp vanilla extract

Place your ice cream churning bowl in the freezer at least 1 day in advance so it is ice cold when you are ready to churn your ice cream.

Place eggs, maple syrup, kefir, double cream and vanilla extract into a blender then blend on a high speed for 2 minutes until smooth.

Add the mixture directly to the chilled ice cream maker and churn for about 45 minutes. Once churned, transfer the ice cream to a large freezer-safe container and use a spoon to smooth the top. Cover and freeze until the ice cream is firm. Leave out for 5 to 10 minutes before serving to soften.

The ice cream will keep in the freezer for up to 14 days.

WATER KEFIR

The bacteria present in the water kefir culture produce small, gelatine-like crystals called water kefir grains or tibicos. Water kefir grains are said to have originated in Mexico where they apparently appeared as crystals on the paddles of a cactus plant. The grains themselves are a polysaccharide created by the bacteria and yeast which then consume the sugar in the water.

These small crystals turn sugar water into a bubbly, fermented drink which is a great and refreshing alternative to fizzy drinks. All you need are the water kefir grains and sugar water. After fermentation, the water kefir can be transferred into bottles for a secondary phase of fermentation with some added fruit.

The fruit will add flavour and colour to the water kefir, and will also produce a slight fizz as the sugar in the fruit ferments. To stop the fermentation process, transfer the water kefir to the fridge and enjoy at your leisure!

Make sure to taste the water kefir at different stages of the fermentation process to see what flavours you prefer. For a sweeter flavour, shorten the fermentation time. The flavour will become more acidic as more sugar is fermented by the grains over time.

One big difference between water kefir and kombucha is the length of time it takes to brew a batch. Water kefir only requires about 2 days of fermentation, unlike kombucha which typically requires between 7 to 30 days to brew.

HOW TO MAKE
WATER KEFIR

1L filtered water
3-4 tbsp unrefined cane sugar
3-4 tbsp water kefir grains
1 thumb-sized piece of ginger, peeled (optional)
½ lemon (optional)
3 tbsp unsulphured raisins (optional)

First fermentation:

Bring 750ml of the water to the boil over a medium heat, then stir in the sugar until it dissolves. Add the remaining 250ml of cold water. Allow to cool completely before transferring the sugar water to a 1L Kilner jar. Add the water kefir grains, ginger, raisins and lemon to the Kilner jar. Cover your Kilner jar loosely with a cloth and allow the kefir to brew at room temperature for 24 to 72 hours, depending on your taste preference. Leaving your water kefir to brew for longer might starve the water kefir grains. After brewing, strain the water kefir grains, raisins, lemon and ginger from the water kefir using a non-metal strainer.

Second fermentation:

Pour the liquid into 250ml or 330ml bottles and add a piece of fruit for flavour and extra sweetness, which is needed for the second fermentation. Let the bottles rest at room temperature for another 24 to 48 hours to continue the fermentation process and produce natural carbonation. The water kefir grains will feed on the fructose in the piece of fruit and create a pleasant natural fizz. Keep in the fridge to stop the fermentation. Serve cold over ice and enjoy!

The warmer your house is, the faster your water kefir will brew. Be aware that the water kefir can overflow if left outside the fridge for too long.

KOMBUCHA

Kombucha uses a SCOBY which has a jelly consistency and looks like a large brown mushroom. SCOBY stands for Symbiotic Culture Of Bacteria and Yeast.

The main bacteria in a SCOBY is called acetic acid bacteria (AAB), which is readily available in plants, mainly stone fruits like apples, pears and plums. The yeast converts carbohydrates into ethanol (alcohol) and the AAB breaks down the ethanol into ethanoic, or acetic, acid. To make kombucha you need a sweet liquid as a carbohydrate source to feed the bacteria during the fermentation process. This can be sweetened black or green tea, as is traditional in Japan, a fruit juice or any liquid sweetened with a simple sugar.

Kombucha will produce vinegar-like flavours when left to ferment for longer. Usually the alcohol content is below 0.5% and kombucha is considered a non-alcoholic drink.

You can buy or grow a SCOBY yourself to make kombucha. We would recommend buying one as they are fairly inexpensive and much more reliable. With the increased popularity of kombucha more people are selling the culture.

Below are tips how to look out for excellent quality:

Size: the circumference of the SCOBY isn't as important as the depth. A 2cm thickness is ideal. Colour: your SCOBY should be off white or cream. Stay clear of any SCOBY that you can see through as these will not be good enough. Shape: round SCOBYs are much easier to brew with.

If you want to grow your own SCOBY you need to buy some unfiltered, flat kombucha from a local shop. Pour this into a wide rimmed container or a clean bowl. Cover with a cloth and leave at room temperature for 7 to 14 days until a SCOBY has formed. This sounds fairly easy, but due to lack of regulation in the kombucha market it may be difficult to know which kombucha is unfiltered and flat.

HOW TO MAKE
KOMBUCHA

2L filtered water
6 tea bags or 6 tsp loose tea (black, green, white)
200g sugar
1 SCOBY

First fermentation:
Brew the tea of your choice with the filtered water. Use green or jasmine for a lighter taste, black for an earthier, stronger taste. Dissolve the sugar in the tea and let it cool down. Place the SCOBY in the fermentation jar and fill up with the sweetened tea.

The SCOBY should float on the surface, but don't worry if it sinks. Cover the jar with a cloth and leave in a warm area for 4 days. Your kombucha will not be fizzy yet but will taste like classic kombucha. At this point, take out the SCOBY and store in a container in the fridge with some kombucha to preserve it.

CARBONATING AND FLAVOURING YOUR
KOMBUCHA

Second fermentation:
For carbonating you will need a fresh source of carbohydrate such as a syrup or fruit purée, which can be added directly to your kombucha brew. Ideally, you should add 10 to 20% syrup or juice relative to the volume of your kombucha brew.

You will need a few fermentation-grade bottles: these should be 250ml or 330ml, round (corners are a weakness in bottles), brown glass (to stop the sun spoiling your brew) and sealable (with a swing cap).

The process will be contained in the bottle causing the brew to be carbonated and when you release the pressure (remove the lid) the brew will be fizzy. Leave the bottles for about 3 days during the second fermentation process before checking for flavour and fizz.

    NATURAL · FERMENTED · LIVING FOOD

APPLE KOMBUCHA

1L fresh apple juice
100ml kombucha (from first
fermentation on page 42)
1 SCOBY

Pour the apple juice and 100ml of kombucha into the fermentation jar and place the scoby into the liquid. Cover the jar with the cloth and leave the kombucha to ferment 7 to 14 days depending on taste preference.

COFFEE KOMBUCHA

1L freshly brewed coffee
100g sugar
1 SCOBY

Brew the coffee with the filtered water to your preferred strength, add sugar and stir to dissolve, let it cool to room temperature.
Place the SCOBY in the fermentation jar and fill up with the sweetened coffee.
Cover the jar with a cloth and leave in a warm area for 4 days. Once fermented to your liking transfer to bottles and store in the fridge. Store the SCOBY in a container with enough coffee kombucha to keep it submerged, keep in the fridge until next use.

〜 ⚡ 🪷 ◐ ◉   NATURAL • FERMENTED • LIVING FOOD

ORANGE OR MANDARIN KOMBUCHA

1L fresh orange or mandarin juice
100ml kombucha (from first fermentation on page 42)
1 SCOBY

Using the same method for the Apple Kombucha on page 43, ferment 7 to 14 days depending on taste preference. Fermenting fruit juices is considered an 'experimental' kombucha. The fructose of the fruit juice in this fermentation process is the source of carbohydrates for the SCOBY.

High Tip

Kombucha is such a nice alternative to alcohol.
There are so many different flavours.

We've had customers celebrating an engagement, a birthday or a promotion and we would give them a complimentary champagne glass filled with sparkling kombucha. Water kefir or kombucha makes a great gift to take to a dinner party or family occasion.

WILD FERMENTATION

WHAT WE RECOMMEND YOU DO (AND DON'T DO) AT HOME

Now that you know how to make fermented drinks, we will take you on the next step of the journey by showing you how to ferment vegetables.

At High Mood Food, we ferment our vegetables using wild fermentation. This means that fermentation is spontaneously induced by microorganisms living on the vegetables. We prefer to allow the process to go through all stages of fermentation without using bacteria of the later fermentation stages. We do not add starters of any kind, not even the brine of previous ferments.

Fermentation is actually quite a simple process. No special cooking skills are required, just an interest in the topic and some willingness for trial and error.

You will need a few Kilner jars, a good knife, a sharp slicer and some fermentation weights. Kilner jars have a rubber ring between the jar and the cap, allowing for depressurisation during fermentation. Oxygen above the ferment is slowly replaced by carbon dioxide which creates a favourable environment for the bacteria. Sometimes burping the ferment is recommended but we are not keen on opening the jar as it destroys the anaerobic environment that the friendly bacteria worked so hard to create and which protects against mould and other harmful organisms. If there is a build-up of pressure, the ferment tends to become quite noisy!

Some ferments are quieter, but there are other signs that your ferment is doing its job. The brine will slowly turn cloudy and you will see bubbles rising to the surface.

You may be tempted to invest in beautiful fermentation pots, but many fermentation fans prefer glass jars. With Kilner jars you will be able to see the changes in the contents and observe the rate of the fermentation process. This is useful for seeing how long it takes certain combinations to take off. There is also something meditative in watching your work come alive!

Lactic acid bacteria are found in all plants in low quantities, but they multiply quickly as a defence mechanism once harvested. You can ferment almost every plant, but don't expect softer vegetables like courgettes to keep their crunchy texture.

Some vegetables will ferment very quickly and tend to leak, especially when the jar is filled above the shoulder (the curve of the glass). Spillage can happen and tends to be smelly; don't overfill your jar and place it on a plate for safety.

Another phenomenon you may observe is vegetables taking up less space during fermentation while the proportion of brine increases. A classic example is our hot sauce; the different chillies become softer and shrink. This is normal and part of the process: no need to worry. In lacto-acid fermentation a 'baker's percentage' is used. For example, if the recipe calls for 4% then 100g of shredded cabbage would require 4g of sprinkled salt and a 4% brine is 4g of salt dissolved in 100ml of water. The percentage represents how many parts of the total weight or volume will be salt.

Sprinkle the salt directly on the shredded vegetables and massage gently. This will draw out the liquid from the vegetables and produce the brine necessary for the fermentation. Usually there is no need to add any additional liquid, but if the vegetables are reluctant to release enough water a saline solution can be used to top up your jar.

You can use slightly less or more salt than stated in our recipes once you figure out what taste you prefer. Using less salt might encourage the growth of bacteria and more salt will slow down the fermentation time. We recommend natural salt rather than table salt which contains iodine, as we don't want to sanitise and kill off the bacteria after all that effort.

Lastly, remember that under the brine is fine! Whether using the so-called dry or liquid method, all herbs and spices need to be packed in carefully with the vegetables, staying under the surface of the brine to prevent any mould from forming. Put the smallest ingredients like spices at the bottom of your jar, continue with the smaller pieces of vegetables (such as chillies) and finish with the larger and chunkier pieces of vegetables. Lay the fermentation weights on top to ensure that no tiny parts can surface and then fill the jar up with brine, making sure everything is submerged.

High Tip

Your kitchen should be clean but there is no need to sterilise surfaces. We recommend labelling your batches with the date they were made so that you can keep track of the fermentation process.

KRAUT

Kraut is a synonym for sauerkraut, a traditional Central and Eastern European food that was historically eaten with sausages. High has developed some tasty and crunchy recipes that accompany and enhance the taste profile of many different dishes.

These beneficial bacteria produce great flavour by transforming carbohydrates into lactic acid. They are resistant to salt and work their magic without oxygen, creating an environment that is very difficult for harmful bacteria to live in.

Did you Know

Two different methods can be used when fermenting vegetables: the dry or wet method. Kraut is an example of the dry method: the cabbage is massaged with salt and this process draws the liquid from the vegetable which is then used as the brine during the fermentation process. The wet method uses a saltwater solution to fill up the jar for fermenting vegetables that cannot be massaged to produce brine, such as tomatoes, cauliflower or cucumber. These are submerged in saltwater which is added to the jar.

CHRISTMAS KRAUT

1kg red cabbage
20g salt
2 apples, cut into matchsticks
1 cinnamon stick

5 cloves
1 star anise
1 tbsp dried orange peel
1 tsp grated fresh ginger

Wash the cabbage, remove the stems and finely slice the leaves. Massage the sliced cabbage with the salt, until some liquid is released, then mix in the apple matchsticks, spices, orange peel and ginger. Pack the kraut into a 1L Kilner jar, making sure that there is no air between the cabbage leaves. Press down with a fermentation weight. Ferment for at least 4 weeks at room temperature. Move to the fridge to slow down fermentation.

  NATURAL · FERMENTED · LIVING FOOD

CLASSIC KRAUT

1kg white cabbage
20g salt
1 tbsp caraway seeds

Remove the outer leaves and cut the cabbage into quarters. Finely slice the leaves then massage the salt into the cabbage until some liquid is released. Stir in the caraway seeds, then pack the mixture into a 1L Kilner jar, making sure there is no air between the cabbage leaves. Press down with a fermentation weight. Ferment for at least 4 weeks at room temperature, covered with a brown bag.

High Tip: toasting the caraway seeds in a hot, dry pan before adding them to the cabbage will intensify the flavour.

CURRIED KRAUT

1kg white kraut
2 large carrots, coarsely grated
1 large onion, sliced
1 tbsp grated fresh ginger

30g salt
2 tbsp curry powder
1 tbsp grated fresh turmeric
or 1 tbsp ground turmeric

Remove the outer leaves and cut the cabbage into quarters.
Finely slice the leaves and combine all the ingredients in a large bowl. Massage the mixture until the salt draws out some liquid. Pack into a 1.5L Kilner jar making sure that there are no air pockets. Press down with a fermentation weight. Ferment for at least 4 weeks at room temperature.

Did you Know

Did you know: vitamin B is sensitive to UV light, so we recommend placing your jar somewhere dark or covering it with a brown paper bag.

KIMCHI

Kimchi is a staple in Korean cuisine and dates back at least two thousand years. Fermented foods were widely available and documented in ancient historical texts. Kimchi became even more prevalent as Buddhism spread and people followed a vegetarian diet.

The fermentation of vegetables was an ideal method, prior to refrigerators, for preserving the lifespan of foods. In Korea, kimchi was made during the winter by fermenting vegetables in traditional brown ceramic pots and burying them in the ground. At High Mood Food we love the spicy kick of our kimchi recipes, but you can leave out or reduce the chilli for a less spicy, but nonetheless tasty version.

HIGH KIMCHI

1kg Chinese or napa cabbage (approximately 2 small ones)
50g salt
250g carrots, coarsely grated
300g mooli or daikon radish, cubed
1 bunch of spring onions, sliced

Kimchi paste:
1 tbsp fish sauce
1 tbsp grated fresh ginger
2 tbsp Korean chilli flakes
3 cloves of garlic

Remove the base of the cabbages, cut them into quarters
then slice each quarter into 2cm strips.
Sprinkle the cabbage with the salt and gently massage it in, then cover with cold water
to make a brine and leave for 2 hours or overnight. Drain and rinse the cabbage.

Combine all the ingredients for the paste and blend until smooth. Combine
the prepared cabbage with the paste, carrots, mooli or daikon and
spring onions then transfer the mixture to a 1.5 or 2L Kilner jar.

Compress the vegetables until everything is under the brine, then
place a fermentation weight on top and close the jar.

Keep the kimchi at room temperature, out of direct sunlight,
for 5 days and then transfer to the fridge.

Did you Know

In 2013, kimchi was listed as an Intangible Cultural Heritage of Humanity.
Kimchi is an essential part of Korean meals and identity. Preparation
follows a yearly cycle and knowledge is often shared between the women
in families, creating a strong sense of community.

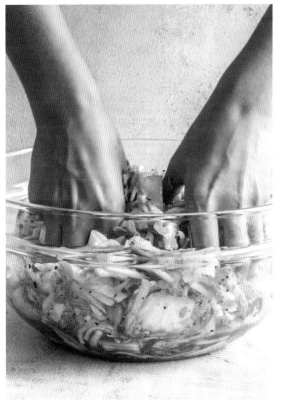

≋ ⚡ ⚘ ⊛ ◉   NATURAL · FERMENTED · LIVING FOOD

GREEN KIMCHI

1.3kg Chinese or napa cabbage (approximately 2 medium ones)
55g salt
400g mooli or daikon radish, cubed
1 bunch of spring onions, sliced

Kimchi paste:
Handful of fresh coriander
15g kelp flakes, or any other seaweed
2 lemongrass stalks, chopped
3 green chillies, deseeded and sliced
1 tbsp grated fresh ginger
2 tbsp water
3 cloves of garlic

Remove the base of the cabbages, cut them into quarters then slice each quarter into 2cm strips. Sprinkle the cabbage with the salt and gently massage it in, then cover with cold water to make a brine and leave for 2 hours or overnight. Drain and rinse the cabbage.

Combine all the ingredients for the paste and blend until smooth. Combine the prepared cabbage with the paste, mooli or daikon and spring onions then transfer the mixture to a 2L Kilner jar.

Compress the vegetables until everything is under the brine, then place a fermentation weight on top and close the jar.

Keep the kimchi at room temperature, out of direct sunlight, for 5 days and then transfer to the fridge.

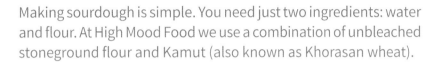

KAMUT
ANCIENT GRAIN SOURDOUGH

Making sourdough is simple. You need just two ingredients: water and flour. At High Mood Food we use a combination of unbleached stoneground flour and Kamut (also known as Khorasan wheat).

The natural yeasts in the grains are activated with the water and these yeasts feed on the carbohydrates in the flour.

This produces carbon dioxide and acetic lactic acid which gives the bread its typical sour flavour.

You can make your own starter or ask your local bakery for some of theirs. The older the starter, the stronger the yeasts are likely to be, which will yield a better bread.

We use Kamut flour, as ancient grains are in a more natural form compared to modern wheat which could have been genetically modified and highly processed. Ancient grains tend to be higher in fibre, protein and vitamins.

Kamut is rich in polyphenols and fatty acids, as well as minerals like selenium, which are shown to support a healthy immune system.

MAKING A SOURDOUGH LOAF

Equipment you're going to need:

Kitchen scale
Proving basket (or a bowl lined with a clean linen cloth)
Dough scraper
Sharp knife
Cast iron pot or a ceramic baking tray
Stand mixer with a dough hook (optional, but will make the process much easier)

If you don't have a stand mixer it's best to knead your dough by
hand using the 'fold and slap' method: fold the dough from corner
to corner then throw it onto your counter making a slapping sound.

KAMUT SOURDOUGH BREAD

100g Kamut (Khorasan) flour
300g bread flour
360g warm water
2-3 tbsp sourdough starter
10g sea salt flakes

In the mixing bowl, combine the flours with the water and sourdough starter on a low speed. Slowly increase the speed and mix for 10 minutes. Then add the salt and mix for an additional 5 minutes. Wrap the bowl in cling film and place in your fermentation area (a room at ambient temperature) for 2 hours. After this time your dough should have risen.

Place the dough onto a floured surface then knead until it has a smooth consistency. At this stage you can fold in some herbs, activated nuts or seeds to give the bread extra crunch and flavour. Cover with a cloth and allow it to rest for another hour, then knead the dough again, working more gently as the dough becomes elastic. Repeat the process until the dough feels smooth and bouncy. It is now ready to be shaped!

First, flour your proving basket. Pull all the corners of your dough into the centre and pinch them together to create a seam. This will tighten up the outside of your loaf, forming a solid crust. Place the dough in your proving basket with the seam facing upwards. Leave in the fridge for 12 hours. Take your dough out of the fridge 4 hours before you plan on baking it.

Preheat your oven to 220ºc with your cast iron pot or baking tray inside. Pull the hot pot or tray out of the oven, lightly flour it and then turn your bread onto it with the seam facing down. Score the top in one quick slice.

Place the pot or tray back into the oven, and put an ovenproof dish half filled with water on the bottom of the oven to create steam. This will give you the chewy crust which is a mark of good sourdough. Bake at 220ºc for 10 minutes and then turn the oven down to 180ºc and bake for another 40 minutes. To check whether your bread is done, tap the base of the loaf. If it sounds hollow, it's ready. Allow your sourdough to cool for 20 minutes or so, as it will continue cooking and needs to rest before being sliced.

BREAK YA FAST

Your first meal of the day

Some people need a big breakfast and perhaps prefer to eat the same thing every morning, while others don't really get hungry until mid-morning. It is an opportunity to check in with yourself and what your gut needs. Once your gut bacteria are used to the 5 K, you might even feel like incorporating kimchi into your breakfast!

We like to treat breakfast as the first meal of the day, whether you choose to eat early in the morning or later. We believe intermittent fasting for 12 to 14 hours or longer can help support the digestive system and allow it to recharge.

Our breakfast recipes are also versatile: our omelette, for examaple, can be a great choice for lunch or dinner, and our Bircher slow and steady seed pot is a great energy boost in the afternoon.

Mix and match your breakfast dishes throughout the day and have an immunity boosting High Flyer or smoothie as a pick-me-up in the afternoon!

HIGH DRINKS

Have a High drink and keep calm and nourished!

Our shots, teas and lattes are carefully crafted to provide you with nutrients throughout the day.

BEETROOT SHOT

2 raw beetroot
10ml lime juice
Knob of ginger

Juice all of the ingredients together. Enjoy as a shot.

CELERY AND CUCUMBER SHOT

A few sticks of organic celery
½ cucumber
Handful of mint

Juice the celery, cucumber and mint together. Enjoy straight
away for an early morning energy boost!

GRAPEFRUIT AND CBD SHOT

½ grapefruit
2-3 drops 10% CBD oil

Juice the grapefruit. Add the juice and the CBD oil to a blender and blitz until
combined. For more fibre in our grapefruit shot, try blending the pulp with
the juice and CBD oil. Keep a few in the fridge as a refreshing booster!

IMMUNITY BOOST SHOT

50ml coconut water
½ lemon
Knob of ginger, peeled
Small knob of fresh turmeric, peeled
Pinch of bee pollen
Pinch of black pepper

Blend all the ingredients together. Strain the liquid through a sieve, decant into
glasses and add extra pinches of bee pollen and black pepper to taste.

    NATURAL · FERMENTED · LIVING FOOD

KIMCHI SHOT

Use some extra brine from your kimchi to prepare a few shots and have them ready to go in the fridge. These are an excellent boost for your digestion with lots of good bacteria!

5 K SHOT

The 5 K shot is High's signature booster to start your day, with a variety of different beneficial bacteria. We believe that your tummy will get a great boost from the cultures of five different ferments and be able to cope better with whatever you choose to eat throughout the day!

10ml kombucha
10ml kefir water
10ml beetroot and Kamut sourdough kvass
10ml kimchi brine
10ml kraut brine

Strain the kimchi and kraut brines. Mix all of the ingredients together. Serve cold.
Try out different combinations of kombucha, kefir water and brines to create new flavors
for your 5K shots.

  NATURAL • FERMENTED • LIVING FOOD

HOW TO MAKE KVASS
It's another K!

Beet kvass and bread kvass are two different drinks. Kvass is a traditional Eastern European beverage that was originally made by fermenting sourdough bread. Beet kvass is salty and made by fermenting beets. The kvass in our High recipe is a mixture of both.

100g sugar
20g salt
1L filtered water
½ loaf of sourdough,
cubed and toasted (stale
is fine just not mouldy)
2 beetroot, peeled and grated

Dissolve the sugar and salt in the filtered water. Place the toasted bread and grated beetroot in a fermentation vessel.

Fill up your jar with the salt and sugar brine, making sure everything is submerged. Cover the jar with a cheesecloth.

Ferment for 7 days at a consistent temperature, ideally 30°c. Pass the mixture through muslin cloth into a clean jar and chill.

Kvass typically lasts for at least a week in the fridge, but it will lose sweetness and become more carbonated the longer it is chilled.

High Tip

If you like your kvass fizzier (more carbonated) just add a few raisins after straining, put a tight lid on and let it ferment at ambient temperature for another day or two.

  NATURAL • FERMENTED • LIVING FOOD

IMMUNITY BOOST

This makes 850ml of concentrate that can be kept in the fridge.
Mix with hot water or enjoy more intensely as a shot.

250g ginger, peeled
250ml honey
125ml lemon juice
1 tsp cayenne pepper

Add all of the ingredients to a blender. Blend for a few minutes until the mixture has a thick consistency. Use the back of a spoon to press the mixture through a sieve.

Bottle this concentrate and store in the fridge, where it will last for up to a month. Mix 25ml of the concentrate with 175ml of hot water to enjoy as a warming drink.

ALKALISER

150ml hot water
1 tsp lemon juice
1 tsp coconut oil

Either stir the ingredients together with a spoon or, for a frothier drink, use a blender to whizz them up.

APPLE CIDER CLEANSE

200ml live apple cider vinegar
100ml honey
½ tsp ground cinnamon

Combine all the ingredients in a blender until smooth.
To drink, mix 2 tablespoons of the concentrate with hot water, adjusting the amount to taste.
The concentrate can be stored in the fridge for up to 2 weeks.

RED CAPPUCCINO

Rooibos tea leaves or capsules
Milk of your choice
Ground cinnamon, for sprinkling

Red cappuccinos can be made in an espresso machine, using
capsules of rooibos tea, or with strong rooibos tea leaves brewed
in a cafetiere. Mix with your milk of choice and sprinkle a little
cinnamon on top. Homemade almond milk is our favourite.

    NATURAL • FERMENTED • LIVING FOOD

  NATURAL · FERMENTED · LIVING FOOD

TURMERIC LATTE MIX

Makes about 3 servings

50g coconut sugar
20g ground turmeric
10g ground cinnamon
1 tsp ground ginger
1 tsp lucuma powder
1 tsp maca powder
¼ tsp black pepper
1 cardamom pod
175ml hot water or milk of your choice

Blend all the dry ingredients to a fine powder, either in a blender or with a mortar and pestle. Add 25g of the powder to 175ml of hot water or milk of your choice and combine with a whisk. Store the remaining powder in an airtight container. Sprinkle a little ground cinnamon on top of your latte for an extra special touch.

Did you Know

Researchers praise a long list of turmeric's benefits: from cancer to depression, Alzheimer's disease to eye health, the spice seems to be proving beneficial as an all-round preventative agent and an incredible anti-inflammatory. Consuming black pepper with turmeric increases the bioavailability of curcumin, its main active ingredient, as per a report in the National Center for Biotechnology Information, US.

MATCHA LATTE

1 tsp high grade matcha
175ml hot water or milk of your choice

Make a paste with the matcha and a little hot water. Whisk vigorously in a zig zag motion until the tea is frothy. Slowly stir your preferred warmed milk into the paste.

Make a paste with the matcha and a little hot water. Whisk in an anti-clockwise motion until it forms a smooth paste, preferably using a matcha whisk but anything you have is fine. Slowly stir in your preferred warm milk or water into the paste then decorate with a sprinkle of matcha powder.

 NATURAL · FERMENTED · LIVING FOOD

MACA HOT CHOCOLATE

This recipe makes about three portions of the dry mix, which can be stored and enjoyed with hot water or milk of your choice.

50g cocoa powder
25g coconut sugar
25g maca powder
Pinch of ground cinnamon
Pinch of sea salt

Sieve all of your ingredients into a bowl. Mix well and store in an airtight container. For a delicious hot chocolate, mix about 2 tablespoons of the powder with 1 cup of hot water or your milk of choice.

BULLET COFFEE

Our bullet coffee contains a high amount of healthy saturated fats, which are beneficial for our brains. In addition to the creamy taste and texture, bullet coffees have been associated with improved metabolism, weight loss and increased mood and strength.

1 double shot of espresso
20g butter
20g coconut oil

Blend all the ingredients together in a blender until smooth. This process cools the coffee slightly so you might want to add some hot water.

For extra caffeine-free flavour, add a spoonful of chicory powder or a similar alternative to your bullet coffee.

   NATURAL · FERMENTED · LIVING FOOD

HIGH-DRATION

Handful of baby spinach
A few mint leaves
½ cucumber
½ lime, juiced
250ml coconut water

Wash the baby spinach and blend it with the mint, cucumber, lime juice and coconut water. Strain through a sieve and enjoy cold.

Natural separation can occur so simply stir when you are ready to drink.

ACV LEMONADE

1 tbsp honey
200ml water
Knob of ginger, peeled
½ lemon, juiced
2 tbsp unpasteurised apple cider vinegar

Dissolve the honey in the water by whisking them together in a jug. Chop the ginger into matchsticks then add to the jug along with the lemon juice and apple cider vinegar. Combine all the ingredients then chill the lemonade until ready to drink.

PREBIOTIC
POWER SMOOTHIE

Makes 1-2 servings

220ml almond milk
50ml kefir
25g ground flax seed
½ banana, peeled
Handful of spinach
½ tsp vanilla extract
2 ice cubes

Blend all the ingredients together until smooth then serve immediately.

High Tip

Depending on your training goals, you could add one or two spoonfuls
of coconut oil, avocado or almond butter to add some healthy fats.

NATURAL • FERMENTED • LIVING FOOD

BREAKFAST BOWLS

Easy to prepare the night before and enjoy in the morning;
our breakfast bowls will gear you up for the day ahead!

FRUIT COMPOTE

Compotes can be made from almost any fruit and are a great way to
use up bruised or slightly overripe fruit, reducing food waste.

6 apples (use a combination
of Bramleys, Galas and
Granny Smiths)
200g blackberries
100g raspberries

100g blueberries
2 grapefruits, zested and juiced
1 lemon, zested and juiced
2 star anise
1 cinnamon stick

Core and cut your selected apples into even pieces. Add them to a saucepan with the rest
of the ingredients. Cook on a low heat for about 15 to 20 minutes until the fruit is tender.
Discard the cinnamon stick and star anise. Allow the mixture to cool
before storing. It keeps in the fridge for a week and freezes well.

CHIA PUDDING

Makes 2-3 servings

50g cracked chia seeds
200ml almond milk
100g coconut or dairy yoghurt
10g maple syrup (optional)
½ tsp vanilla extract

Mix the chia seeds and almond milk together directly in the jar or bowl. You might need a little more liquid depending on the consistency and how much the chia seeds absorb. Add the coconut yoghurt, maple syrup and vanilla extract, mix well then leave in the fridge overnight. This will keep in the fridge for up to 2 days. Serve with our Paleo Granola (see page 95) and Fruit Compote (see opposite).

Did you Know

Chia seeds are so nutritionally valuable that they were once used as currency. These tiny black or white seeds swell into gelatinous mousse when mixed with liquids, and are powerful endurance and energy agents loved by athletes, sometimes called 'runners' food!' They're very low in calories and you can add them to smoothies or any breakfast. Remember to crack or blend the seeds first for better swelling and absorption.

≋ ⚡ 🪷 🌿 👁 NATURAL · FERMENTED · LIVING FOOD

BIRCHER MUESLI

This is a super easy dish that keeps for a few days and is ideal for a quick, nutritious breakfast. Soaking the oats and seeds overnight makes them easier to digest, and the muesli will be extra creamy.

Makes about 4 servings

2 apples
300ml almond milk (or another milk of your choice)
150g gluten-free oats
50g coconut yogurt
1 lemon, juiced
½ tsp ground cinnamon

Grate the apples on the coarse side of a box grater. Mix them with all the remaining ingredients in a bowl. Transfer everything into an airtight container and leave to soak overnight in the fridge.

High Tip

Although we advise caution when adding sweeteners, a spoonful of local honey can help fight pollen allergies because the bees collect pollen sourced from local plants. Since many seasonal allergies are caused by these same plants, eating honey which contains that pollen can possibly help to fight those allergies. The idea of exposing patients with food allergies to trace amounts of the allergens in order to desensitise them is gaining traction. In addition to potentially fighting allergies, one of the great benefits of local honey is that it's unprocessed and pure.

SLOW AND STEADY SEEDS

This will make about 4 servings and can be kept in the fridge for up to 2 days.

1 apple	50g pumpkin seeds
400g kefir	40g ground flax seeds
50g chia seeds	1 tsp vanilla extract
50g sunflower seeds	Pinch of sea salt

Grate the apple on the coarse side of a box grater. Mix it with the rest of the ingredients in a bowl. Transfer everything into an airtight container and soak overnight in the fridge. Serve with a mix of fruit, yoghurt and toasted seeds.

   NATURAL • FERMENTED • LIVING FOOD

ANCIENT GRAIN PORRIDGE

At High Mood Food we prefer to use the grains: millet, barley, teff, oat and sorghum as well as the pseudo-cereals: quinoa, amaranth and buckwheat. Plenty of ancient grains are gluten-free, such as quinoa, millet, fonio, sorghum, amaranth, and teff. You can experiment with your own mix of ancient grains or use our High recipe.

Makes about 4 servings

300ml almond milk
100g gluten-free oats
50g puffed millet
50g coconut yoghurt
20g flax seeds

20g chia seeds
1 tbsp honey
1 grapefruit, zested
1 lemon, juiced
Pinch of salt

Add all the ingredients except the coconut yoghurt to a pan. Slowly bring to the boil and simmer until thickened. The longer it cooks, the more it thickens so add more liquid to your liking. Finish by stirring in the coconut yoghurt, then serve warm with local honey. Top with some delicious seasonal berries or fruit compote (see page 86).

  NATURAL · FERMENTED · LIVING FOOD

FIVE GRAIN, FIVE HERB MISO PORRIDGE

Makes about 4 servings

200g ancient grains (we use
black quinoa, buckwheat,
amaranth, red rice and spelt)
350ml water
2 tbsp dark miso
2 tbsp extra virgin olive oil
Handful of fresh herbs (we
use mint, basil, parsley,
coriander and chives)

Toppings:
1 aubergine
1 tbsp dark miso
2 tbsp extra virgin olive oil
1 tsp white or black sesame seeds
A few chives, finely chopped
eggs, poached (optional,
see page 99)

Soak the ancient grains overnight. Drain and rinse the soaked grains then put them in a saucepan with the water. Bring to the boil then turn the heat down to a simmer for 10 to 12 minutes until the water has been absorbed. In a separate bowl, combine the miso with the olive oil, adding a touch of water if needed to make a smooth paste. Stir this into the grain mix until completely coated. Finely chop the herbs of your choice, fold them through the ancient grains and season with a pinch of salt.

Preheat the oven 200 °c while you cut the aubergine into 2cm slices. Mix the miso and olive oil together into a smooth paste, brush this over both sides of the aubergine slices and place them on a baking tray lined with greaseproof paper. Place in the preheated oven and roast for 12 to 15 minutes, turning halfway through so each side cooks evenly. Serve the miso porridge topped with the roasted aubergine and sprinkled with sesame seeds and chives.

PALEO GRANOLA

At High Mood Food we activate all of our nuts and seeds to reduce the phytic acid content, which can trigger bloating by limiting the activity of several digestive enzymes, and when consumed in large quantities can cause mineral deficiencies. We use the process of soaking them in saltwater for 8 to 12 hours. Once activated, the nuts and seeds are dried at a very low temperature (under 65°c) in a dehydrator, to crisp them back up as well as keeping them raw and full of beneficial enzymes.

If you do not have a dehydrator at home, you can use your oven on a very low temperature of around 60 to 65°c and dry the nuts overnight.

Makes a batch of about 750g

150g coconut flakes
150g flaked almonds
150g activated almonds
150g activated sunflower seeds
100g activated pumpkin seeds
15g chia seeds
3 tbsp maple syrup
3 tbsp coconut oil
2 tbsp vanilla extract
1 tsp ground cinnamon
1 tsp ground ginger
½ tsp sea salt

Preheat the oven to 140°c. Mix all the ingredients together in a bowl. Spread the granola out on a flat tray and bake for 2 hours in the preheated oven. Make sure the mixture is an even layer on the tray so that it cooks evenly. Check every 30 minutes and gently stir with a wooden spoon to allow a light golden roast throughout. Once the granola has cooled completely, store in an airtight container for up to about 2 weeks.

SUPERCHARGED EGGS

Eggs easily qualify as a superfood.

They are nutrient-dense and contain all the essential amino acids in addition to omega 3 acids, folate, vitamins B, D, E, and K2 as well as flavonoids and the lesser known choline.

The amounts of these nutrients vary considerably depending on the food you eat eggs with and the living conditions of the laying hens. We recommend the consumption of free-range pastured eggs whenever possible.

BOILED EGGS

Fresh eggs, at room temperature
1L boiling water
1 tbsp white wine vinegar

Put the litre of water and the vinegar in a large saucepan and bring to the boil. Gently lower in your eggs and set the timer. For a soft boiled egg, cook for 4.5 minutes. For a slightly harder boiled egg with a fudgy yolk, cook for 6 minutes. For a hard boiled egg, cook for about 7.5 minutes. The exact time depends on the size of the egg. If you are eating the egg cold with lunch or canapes, drop the egg into ice water immediately. This stops the cooking process and makes the egg easier to peel. Skip this step if you are eating the boiled eggs straightaway, and serve hot.

SCRAMBLED EGGS

3 eggs
20g butter
Sea salt and black pepper
Double cream (optional)

Whisk the eggs in a bowl. Add the butter to a small non-stick saucepan on a medium heat. Add the beaten egg and let it sit for about 20 seconds without stirring. Once it is set, gently scramble using a spatula. If you like, add some double cream at this stage. Remove from the heat and season with salt and pepper to serve.

High Tip

To give your morning a gut-healthy start, add some vegetables, kimchi or kraut!

POACHED EGGS

Fresh eggs, at room temperature
2L boiling water
3 tbsp white wine vinegar

Crack each egg into a separate bowl or saucer. Pour the boiling water and vinegar into a large pan (ideally it should be deeper than it is wide). Heat gently until bubbles start to appear. Using a slotted spoon or fork, spin the water until a vortex appears. Tip each egg into the swirling water one at a time, making sure to drop them at the edge of the pan. Cook for 4.5 minutes for a runny yolk. Remove from the pan using a slotted spoon.

OMELETTE

3 eggs
1 tbsp butter
Sea salt and black pepper
Grated cheese (optional)

Over a medium heat, melt the butter in a small non-stick pan. Meanwhile, gently whisk the eggs in a bowl. Pour the eggs into the pan and evenly distribute them using a spatula. Allow the eggs to set slightly and then gently pull the set edges into the centre of the pan. Season with salt and pepper, and, if you want to add grated cheese, scatter it over the egg at this point. Allow the omelette to cook for about another minute before folding it in half. Brush the top with a tiny bit more butter for a shiny finish.

TURKISH EGGS

CALM
HIGHLY RELAXING

This dish is great for the weekends when you want something hot and filling but not too heavy to start your day.

Makes 2 servings

4 eggs, poached (see page 99)
200g full-fat Greek yoghurt
2 tbsp extra virgin olive oil
1 large clove of garlic, crushed or grated
½ lemon, zested and juiced
Sea salt, to taste
1 tbsp Simple 'Living' Hot Sauce (see page 176)
1 tbsp Activated Dukkha (see page 184)
1 tbsp hemp seeds
2 slices of sourdough, grilled or freshly baked

Combine the yoghurt, half the olive oil, the garlic, lemon zest and lemon juice with a pinch of salt in a small bowl. Use a large spoon to divide the yoghurt sauce between two plates and spread it out rustically using the back of the spoon.

Lay the poached eggs on top of the sauce, then drizzle generously with the remaining olive oil and Simple 'Living' Hot Sauce to your taste. Top with the Activated Dukkah and hemp seeds then serve with the sourdough.

NATURAL · FERMENTED · LIVING FOOD

KETO BREAKFAST

This is a favourite at the café and makes a delicious quick and easy midweek breakfast. It is packed with healthy fats and lots of beneficial bacteria.

Makes 2 servings

1 large ripe avocado
½ lemon, juiced
Chilli flakes, to taste
100g hot smoked salmon
150g Curried Kraut (see page 53)
4 eggs, poached (see page 99)
2 tbsp extra virgin olive oil, or your favourite plant oil (we also love hemp and avocado oil)
1 tbsp hemp seeds
1 tbsp Activated Tamari Seeds (see page 182)

Scoop out the avocado flesh and place in a small bowl with the lemon juice. Using the back of a fork, mash the avocado then season with chilli flakes, salt and pepper.

Divide the smashed avocado, hot smoked salmon and Curried Kraut between two plates, and place two poached eggs on each one.

Top each dish with a generous drizzle of your favourite plant oil, the hemp seeds and Miso-Tamari Seeds for an umami crunch.

SHAKSHUKA

This is our take on the traditional Middle Eastern breakfast classic. Shakshuka eggs are lovely and warming on a cold winter's morning. We love dipping a slice of toasted sourdough into the rich tomato sauce! You will need a frying pan with a metal handle or a ceramic dish that can go straight from the oven to the table.

Makes 2 servings

1 tbsp extra virgin olive oil
1 red onion, sliced
½ clove of garlic, sliced
½ chilli, deseeded and chopped
1 tsp tomato paste
250g good quality jarred chopped tomatoes
4 eggs
100g feta cheese
1 lemon, zested
1 tbsp coriander, chopped
1 tbsp parsley, chopped

Preheat the oven to 190°c. Heat an ovenproof frying pan on a low heat and add the olive oil. Soften the onion, garlic and chilli with a pinch of salt in the pan for about 1 minute, then add the tomato paste and cook for 2 to 3 minutes. Add the chopped tomatoes and let the sauce simmer until slightly thickened. Make small wells for each egg with a spoon where they can fit snugly and then crack the eggs into the dips.

Place the pan directly into the preheated oven and cook for 5 minutes. Crumble the feta over the shakshuka and cook for another 3 minutes or until the eggs are just set.

Remove from the oven and place a lid on the pan. The steam will cook the eggs through in about 2 minutes. If you prefer your eggs cooked more, leave the lid on for a bit longer and if you prefer a runnier egg you can skip this step.

Garnish the shakshuka with the herbs, lemon zest and a drizzle of olive oil.

GOOD GUT BREAD

Our Good Gut Bread has been a firm favourite from the beginning! We like to serve it with one of our nourishing soups (see page 115), as a base for an open sandwich (see page 108), or simply with cultured butter and local honey. The loaf will keep in the fridge for 5 days, or to ensure you always have a slice handy, preserve its freshness by slicing and placing in the freezer to toast and top at any time!

Makes 1 loaf

200g buckwheat flour
100g ground almonds
60g ground flax seeds
60g sunflower seeds, soaked
or activated (see page 18)
60g pumpkin seeds, soaked
or activated (see page 18)

20g psyllium husk
1 tsp baking powder
½ tsp salt
400ml water
60ml olive oil
1½ tbsp apple cider vinegar

Preheat the oven to 180°c and grease a 23 x 13 x 8cm tin.

In a large bowl, combine the buckwheat flour, ground almonds, ground flax seed, activated sunflower and pumpkin seeds, psyllium husk, baking powder and salt. Mix well. Combine the wet ingredients (water, olive oil and apple cider vinegar) in a separate bowl, then pour this mixture into the dry ingredients.

Use a spoon to incorporate the liquid and create a thick batter-like texture. Add 1 or 2 tablespoons of water if the dough seems too dry. Immediately transfer the dough to a loaf tin. Smooth the top with a wet spatula, drizzle with olive oil, and sprinkle a small handful of sprouted pumpkin and sunflower seeds on top. Lightly push the seeds into the loaf with the spatula so they don't burn.

Place the loaf in the preheated oven to bake for 1 hour and 10 minutes. When the top is nicely coloured, remove from the oven and cool your bread in the tin for at least 10 minutes before transferring to a cooling rack.

BERRY BLAST

1 slice of Good Gut Bread, toasted (see page 107)
1 tbsp hazelnut butter, or your favourite nut butter
1 tbsp coconut yoghurt
1 tbsp fruit compote (see page 86)
1 tsp ground cinnamon
30g seasonal fresh berries
2 tsp cocoa nibs

Spread the toasted Good Gut Bread with the hazelnut butter, then add the coconut yoghurt and fruit compote. Sprinkle with cinnamon, assemble your berries, and top with cocoa nibs.

AVO SMASH

Makes 1 open sandwich

½ large ripe avocado
2 tsp lime juice
Sea salt and black pepper
1 slice of Good Gut Bread, toasted (see page 107)
50g Curried Kraut (see page 53)
2 radishes, finely sliced
1 tbsp hemp seeds
1 tbsp extra virgin olive oil

Scoop the avocado flesh into a bowl and mash with the back of a fork. Add the lime juice and salt and pepper to taste. Spread the avocado on top of the toasted Good Gut Bread. Top with the Curried Kraut, sliced radishes, hemp seeds, a squeeze of fresh lime juice and a drizzle of olive oil.

Add a sprinkle of our Activated Tamari Seeds (see page 182) for extra crunch, or top with a poached egg (see page 99) for a more substantial meal.

     NATURAL · FERMENTED · LIVING FOOD

NATURAL • FERMENTED • LIVING FOOD

CULTURED TOASTIE

Makes 1 toastie

2 slices of sourdough
25g butter, or cultured butter (see page 33)
1 tbsp miso paste
2 tsp Dijon mustard
50g unpasteurised cheddar, grated
25g sauerkraut (see page 53)

Place a heavy-based pan on a low heat. Butter the sourdough slices on both sides, and in addition to the butter, spread one side of one slice with the miso paste, and one side of the other slice with Dijon mustard.

Lay one slice in your pan, butter-only-side down, then top with the grated cheese and kraut. Place the remaining slice on top, butter-only-side up, to create a sandwich, and then flip the whole toastie to brown the other side. Cook low and slow to create a perfectly melted interior and golden crunchy exterior.

High Tip

To make this delicious toastie vegan, swap the cheddar for your favourite vegan cheese, and spread the bread with a plant-based alternative to butter. For a guaranteed gooey centre, mix the miso paste with your favourite non-dairy cream cheese and spread on the inside of your toastie before adding your kraut and vegan cheese.

HIGH NOON

At High Mood Food we love bowl food.
Even with very healthy ingredients, portion
size is important; a bowl should ideally be
equivalent to your own cupped hands.

Bowls are easy to assemble or prepare the
night before. Cold or warm, a bowl will adapt
to your mood and needs!

GUTSY SOUPS

   NATURAL • FERMENTED • LIVING FOOD

MUSHROOM BROTH

1½ tbsp extra virgin olive oil
1kg chestnut mushrooms, sliced
50g dried ceps
1 onion, sliced
5 cloves of garlic, chopped
2 tbsp dark miso paste

Heat 1 tablespoon of the olive oil in a saucepan on a low heat. Add the chestnut mushrooms and slowly cook until they become brown and slightly crispy. Cover with boiling water, add the dried ceps and simmer.

In a separate frying pan, sweat the onion and garlic on a low heat with the remaining olive oil. Once soft, add this mixture to the mushrooms.

Remove a ladle of broth and place in a small bowl with the miso paste. Stir it in then add the liquid back to the saucepan. Stir to incorporate. Simmer your broth for a further 20 minutes then strain and enjoy hot.

TOM YUM

2 lemongrass stalks, bruised to release the flavour
20g fresh ginger, grated using a microplane
2 chillies
1L mushroom broth (see above)
100ml coconut milk

Sweat the lemongrass, ginger and chilli with a little bit of olive oil in a saucepan on low heat. Add the broth and coconut milk.

Simmer for 20 minutes until the broth is aromatic and lightly spicy. Enjoy hot.

BONE BROTH

If you decide to take on the task of making your own bone broth and have the freezer space, it makes sense to go big! Note that the vegetables will have to be discarded at the end of your cooking time, but will give your broth a nice flavour along the way.

3-4kg mixed beef bones (try to include collagen-rich knuckles and tail bones)
4L water
2 tbsp apple cider vinegar
1 large onion, quartered
1 bulb of garlic, halved crossways
2 bay leaves
1 bunch of parsley
2½ tbsp peppercorns
1 star anise

4 carrots
4 sticks of celery
4 parsley roots
3 yellow beets
1-2 leeks, outer layer discarded
¼ cauliflower
¼ cabbage
1 tbsp sea salt

Preheat the oven to 180°c. Spread the bones out evenly on a flat tray and roast in the oven for 60 minutes until browned, flipping halfway through. Place the roasted bones into the largest stock pot you have and cover with the water, making sure there is at least a four-finger space between the rim of the pot and the water level.

Add the apple cider vinegar and bring to a simmer. Place the onion, garlic, bay leaves, parsley, peppercorns and star anise into a spice ball or a muslin cloth tied with string. Put this infuser into the broth and cook on a low heat for at least 10 hours and up to 24 hours. Skim the foam occasionally.

After at least 8 hours, or no less than 2 hours before you intend to finish your broth, add all the vegetables. No need to peel them, just ensure they are washed thoroughly. Once you are happy with the broth, taste and season with sea salt.

Remove the infuser, bones and vegetables then strain the liquid through a sieve. Pour a cup straightaway, or cool the liquid, cover and refrigerate.

Enjoy this as a simple cup of hot nourishing broth, add to any of your favourite soups to elevate their gut-friendly properties, mix with the cooking liquid for rice or quinoa, or use as the base of a simple ramen with buckwheat or shirataki noodles, a soft boiled egg and vegetables of your choice.

     NATURAL · FERMENTED · LIVING FOOD

CHICKEN BROTH

The following recipe is a broth, not a chicken soup. It will yield a highly nutritious liquid, but most of the ingredients will be thoroughly cooked and mellow in flavour. You know you've made a good one when the broth gels in the fridge.

This signifies a high content of gelatin and collagen, which contains easily absorbed amino acids and can aid in healing the lining of the gut. You can achieve this by using good quality bones that have a high amount of cartilage, particularly joints, and by cooking your chicken bones for at least 8 hours in total, but no more than 24 hours.

1.5-2kg chicken bones
(carcasses, neck, wings, even
feet if you can get hold of them)
5L water
A dash of apple cider vinegar
1 small onion
1 clove of garlic
1 bunch of parsley

2 carrots
2 yellow beets
2 parsley roots
½ kohlrabi
5-10 peppercorns
Sea salt, to taste

Preheat the oven to 180°c. Spread the chicken bones evenly onto a baking tray and place in the oven for 45 to 60 minutes to roast. Flip halfway through, and remove from the oven when golden brown. Place the bones into a large stock pot and cover with the water. Add the apple cider vinegar and bring to a simmer. Place the onion, garlic and bunch of parsley in a spice ball or a muslin cloth tied with string. Put this infuser into the broth and simmer on a low heat for 4 to 6 hours. Skim the foam occasionally.

After 4 to 6 hours, add the vegetables. No need to peel, just wash well and roughly chop, then let the broth simmer for another 2 hours. Towards the end, add the peppercorns (if you do this too early, your broth may have a spicy aftertaste) and season with salt. After around 8 hours total cooking time, your broth should be a beautiful clear brown colour. Taste and season to your liking and remove from the heat. Remove the spice ball, bones and vegetables, then strain the broth through a sieve. Cool the liquid down, cover and refrigerate.

   NATURAL • FERMENTED • LIVING FOOD

DAHL

To prepare the red lentils, rinse them under cold running water, then tip them into a pot and cover with recently boiled water. The warm water will help to break down indigestible starches. Add 2 tablespoons of an acid, such as lemon juice or apple cider vinegar, for each cup of lentils. Soak for 8 to 12 hours.

Makes 4 servings

1 tbsp extra virgin olive oil
1 onion, sliced
2 cloves of garlic, chopped
1½ tbsp madras curry powder
1 lemongrass stalk, bruised
1 tbsp tomato puree
200g jarred or tinned chopped tomatoes
200g red lentils, soaked overnight (see instructions above)
100ml coconut milk
2-3 tbsp coconut yoghurt
½ bunch of fresh coriander, chopped

Add the olive oil to a large saucepan on low heat then sweat the onion and garlic. Once softened, add the curry powder and lemongrass. Cook for about 5 minutes, making sure not to burn the spices.

Stir in the tomato puree and chopped tomatoes, then drain and rinse the soaked lentils and add them to the pan. Stir to combine everything then add the coconut milk and 200ml of boiling water. Gently simmer the dahl on a low heat for 15 to 20 minutes until the lentils are cooked to your liking. At this point they should be softened but still hold their shape. To make a creamier dahl, add a little more liquid and cook for longer, or place in a blender and puree until smooth. Stir through the coconut yoghurt to serve. Add an extra dollop on top if desired, and garnish with the fresh coriander.

We love serving ours at the café with a good helping of Curried Kraut (see page 53), a drizzle of Simple 'Living' Hot Sauce (see page 176) and some Activated Dukkah (see page 184).

PUMPKIN SOUP

Makes 2 servings

500g pumpkin, peeled and cubed
1 large red bell pepper, cored and quartered
1 onion, peeled and quartered
4 cloves of garlic, unpeeled
1 sprig of rosemary
1 tbsp olive or coconut oil
Salt and freshly ground black pepper
200ml vegetable stock or hot water
2 tbsp coconut yoghurt

Preheat the oven to 180°c and line a baking tray with greaseproof paper.

Place the chopped pumpkin, red pepper, onion, cloves of garlic and rosemary on the baking tray. Toss with the olive oil and a good pinch of salt then roast in the oven for 30 to 40 minutes until the pumpkin is golden and soft. Make sure the peppers and onions do not burn by stirring the veggies around the tray halfway through cooking. Once caramelised and cooked, remove the vegetables from the oven.

Discard the rosemary, squeeze the cloves of garlic out of their skins and put them into a blender or food processor with the roasted vegetables.

Add the vegetable stock or hot water (you could also use chicken broth (see page 119) for an extra boost of nutrients and flavour) to the blender along with the coconut yoghurt and blend until smooth. Season the soup with salt and black pepper to taste, and serve hot topped with an extra drizzle of coconut yoghurt or olive oil.

We recommend sprinkling some Activated Tamari Seeds (see page 182) over the soup, and adding a slice of toasted Good Gut Bread (see page 107) drizzled with olive oil for a wholesome lunch or dinner.

You could also try adding some Activated Dukkah (see page 184) and Curried Kraut (see page 53) as a topping. If you like a bit of a kick, finish the soup with a drizzle of fermented hot sauce or chilli flakes!

    NATURAL · FERMENTED · LIVING FOOD

JERUSALEM ARTICHOKE SOUP

Makes 2 servings

1 tbsp extra virgin olive oil
1 onion, sliced
2 sticks of celery, chopped
1 clove of garlic
500g Jerusalem artichokes, peeled and cubed
½ tbsp salt, or more to taste
Freshly ground black pepper

Heat the olive oil in a large saucepan and sauté the onion and celery until soft, but not browned. Add the chopped garlic and sauté for a further minute, sprinkle with salt and add the artichokes.

Add enough hot water to cover the vegetables, and boil for around 20 minutes with a lid on until the artichokes are soft.

Transfer all the cooked vegetables and cooking water into a blender or food processor. Blend until smooth, adding more hot water or a drizzle of olive oil until the soup reaches your desired thickness. Season with salt and black pepper to taste. Serve hot.

We recommend serving this soup with our Cultured Toastie (see page 111) for a perfect and comforting gut-happy lunch!

Did you Know

Jerusalem artichokes regularly feature on lists of the best prebiotics for good reason: the tuber contains high levels of inulin, a water soluble polysaccharide which is a great source of prebiotic fibre. Prebiotics are fibres that our friendly gut bacteria feed on. Asparagus, leeks, onions and garlic are other great vegetable sources of inulin.

  NATURAL · FERMENTED · LIVING FOOD

CELERIAC AND HORSERADISH SOUP - WITH A DRIZZLE OF CREAMY KEFIR

Makes 2 servings

1 large celeriac, peeled and grated
50g fresh horseradish, peeled and grated
2 tbsp extra virgin olive oil
2 tbsp kefir (see page 26)
1-2 tsp sea salt

Place your celeriac and salt in a large saucepan and add enough boiling water to cover the vegetable. Bring the heat up to a gentle simmer and stir every 5 minutes. Try not to stir any more as this will break up the celeriac and make it stick to the pan.

Once the celeriac is soft and the water has slightly reduced, transfer to a blender with 1 to 2 tablespoons of grated horseradish and the olive oil. Blend until smooth and creamy.

Season the soup with salt and black pepper to taste, adding a little more horseradish if desired. Serve hot, garnished with a drizzle of kefir and more fresh grated horseradish.

High Tip

This recipe is very simple to make as it only has few ingredients. If you would like to jazz it up, roast the celeriac and a whole bulb of garlic in some olive oil with salt, pepper and a few sprigs of thyme. Blend with some sautéed leeks and vegetable stock to your desired consistency, then garnish with the grated horseradish, a drizzle of kefir, and some chopped roasted hazelnuts.

OUR SALAD BAR

Our High Bowls are veg-centric and at the café we usually combine three salads. You can opt for more carbohydrates in the form of pulses, grains or carb-heavier vegetables, or choose from the low carb options. Add your protein and finish with a kraut or kimchi, a probiotic salad dressing and some activated seeds for a crunchy topping.

We have listed our favourite salad and side recipes which can be treated as nutritional building blocks and planned as a yummy wholesome feast for families and guests with different taste buds. Everybody will find their own composition of fresh and seasonal vegetables, proteins, healthy fats and a variety of gut friendly bacteria from the different ferments.

CURRY ROASTED CAULIFLOWER

1 large cauliflower
100g coconut oil
1 onion
30g garlic
30g fresh ginger

1 lemongrass stalk
4 kaffir lime leaves
1½ tbsp curry powder
40ml Living Hot Sauce (see page 176)

Preheat the oven to 160°c. Wash the cauliflower and pat it dry with a kitchen cloth. Melt the coconut oil in a saucepan. Blend the remaining ingredients together and mix the paste into the melted oil.

Brush the paste onto your cauliflower and place in the oven to roast for around 45 minutes, or until cooked through and golden brown.

     NATURAL · FERMENTED · LIVING FOOD

AYURVEDIC CAULIFLOWER RICE

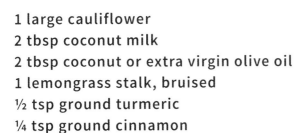

1 large cauliflower
2 tbsp coconut milk
2 tbsp coconut or extra virgin olive oil
1 lemongrass stalk, bruised
½ tsp ground turmeric
¼ tsp ground cinnamon

¼ tsp ground cumin
¼ tsp ground ginger
2 tsp sea salt
1 tbsp lime juice
50g fresh coriander or parsley

Preheat the oven to 180°c. Wash the cauliflower and pat it dry with a kitchen cloth. Use a box grater or pulse in a food processor to break the cauliflower down into rice-sized pieces. You can use the stalk here too. Place the cauliflower rice in a bowl and stir through the coconut milk, oil, lemongrass, ground spices and salt.

Spread the cauliflower rice out flat on a lined baking tray and place in the preheated oven for 6 minutes. Take it out and stir, then return to the oven and cook for another 6 minutes. The cauliflower should begin to look dried out at this point. Leave it to cool on the tray. Once cooled, stir in the lime juice and fresh coriander or parsley then serve.

MISO ROASTED CAULIFLOWER

1 cauliflower
1 tbsp organic miso
2 tsp sesame oil
2 tsp tamari
2 tsp lime juice

Preheat the oven to 160°c. Wash the cauliflower and pat it dry with a kitchen cloth. Trim off the tough outer leaves and discard them.

Mix the miso with the sesame oil, tamari and lime juice to form a paste and brush this onto the whole cauliflower.

Place on a baking tray lined with greaseproof paper and roast for 45 minutes in the preheated oven. The cauliflower will be charred on the outside and soft in the middle. Remove from the oven and let it rest for 10 minutes, then slice open and serve warm or cold.

ALMOST CAESAR SALAD

At High Mood Food, we have our own version of the famous salad by Caesar Cardini, without Worcestershire sauce and using a fermented fish sauce instead of anchovies. Fermented fish sauce is available in most Asian stores or the Asian section of supermarkets. You can replace the egg with 1 or 2 tablespoons of silken tofu.

2 heads of romaine lettuce
1 large egg
3 tbsp lemon juice
75ml extra virgin olive oil
2 tsp fermented fish sauce
1 large or 2 small cloves of garlic, minced or pressed
Freshly ground black pepper, to taste
Sea salt, to taste
40g parmesan or Grana Padano

Cut or tear the lettuce into small pieces, wash, dry and set aside. Bring a samll saucepan of water to the boil. Once the water is boiling, lower the egg in carefully with a spoon so it doesn't crack, and cook for 1 minute. Don't overcook it. You want the egg to be almost raw, while at the same time activating the yolk to end up with a creamy dressing. Transfer the egg straight into a small bowl filled with iced water to cool.

Crack the cooled egg into a medium-size bowl. Whisk the yolk and the egg white together, add the lemon juice, whisk again and slowly add the oil, fish sauce and garlic while whisking continuously. Season the dressing with salt and pepper to taste.

Place the prepared lettuce in a bowl, toss with the dressing and serve with grated or shaved parmesan on top.

For extra creaminess you can also use some full-fat Greek yoghurt in the dressing.

THREE BEANS AND KIMCHI DRESSING

75g butter beans, soaked
75g kidney beans, soaked
75g chickpeas (or garbanzo beans), soaked
50ml Kimchi Dressing (see page 181)
10g fresh coriander, chopped
10g spring onion, chopped

Soak the beans separately. Drain and rinse them under cold water
then combine them in a heavy-based pan with enough cold water to
cover them by 10cm. Bring to the boil and reduce to simmer.

Cook the beans until they are tender. This will take around 1 hour.
Add a pinch of salt at the end and allow the beans to cool in the liquid.
Once the beans have cooled, drain and store in the fridge for up to 2 days until needed.

When ready to serve, dress the beans in the kimchi dressing and
garnish with chopped coriander and spring onion.

BEETROOT, KEFIR
AND FRESH CURD

3-4 large beetroot
A splash of apple cider vinegar
1 tsp sea salt
100g cow's curd (fresh unaged
cheese. If this is unavailable,
ricotta or a mixture of kefir
and yoghurt will also work)
25ml kefir
1 tbsp dill, finely chopped
6 pink radishes, finely sliced

Preheat the oven to 180°c. Wrap each beetroot individually in foil and cook for 45 minutes until tender. Allow to cool then peel with a knife. The skin should come off easily.

While the beetroot is still warm, cut into bite-size pieces and season it with the apple cider vinegar and salt. In a separate bowl, mix the curd with the kefir. Once cool, toss the beetroot with the curd and chopped dill. Finish with dill sprigs and finely sliced pink radishes.

NUTTY SPICED QUINOA
AND BUCKWHEAT

20g buckwheat groats
15g whole almonds, roughly chopped
100g quinoa, soaked for 2 hours in filtered water
200ml vegetable stock
1 tbsp tahini
Extra virgin olive oil
½ tbsp cumin seeds
½ tbsp fennel seeds
1 tsp ground cinnamon
Sea salt, to taste

Preheat the oven 150°c. To toast the buckwheat, rinse and drain the groats and spread them out flat on a baking tray. Place the tray in the oven for 45 minutes until the buckwheat is a toasted amber colour. About halfway through this time, add the chopped almonds and stir the buckwheat, then stir once or twice more to toast the grains and almonds evenly.

Rinse the quinoa until the water runs clear, then drain thoroughly. Bring the vegetable stock to the boil in a saucepan and add the quinoa. Lower the heat to a simmer and cook for about 12 minutes uncovered until tender. Once cooked, transfer the quinoa to a bowl and add the tahini. You may need a tablespoon of olive oil to loosen the paste and stir it through. Chill in the fridge

In a dry pan, toast the cumin and fennel seeds until they start to pop and smell fragrant. When the almonds and buckwheat are golden brown and smelling nutty, remove them from the oven and allow to cool.

Once the quinoa is cold, mix in the buckwheat, almonds, spices and salt. Enjoy chilled.

BLACK TEA QUINOA TABBOULEH

220ml hot water
1-2 black tea bags
100g tricolour quinoa,
soaked for 2 hours
1 tbsp extra virgin olive oil
Sea salt, to taste

1 unwaxed lemon, zested and juiced
4 tbsp pomegranate seeds
½ bunch of parsley, chopped
½ bunch of coriander, chopped
A few sprigs of fresh mint
20g flaked almonds, toasted

Bring the hot water to the boil in a saucepan with the black tea bags and infuse for 5 minutes. Rinse the quinoa until the water runs clear then drain. Remove the tea bags and add the quinoa to the tea, lower the heat and simmer uncovered for about 12 minutes until tender. Once the quinoa is cooked, all the tea should have been absorbed but if not, drain off any residual tea. Stir through the oil and salt while the quinoa is hot and cover.

Leave to cool, or chill in the fridge. When ready to serve, transfer the quinoa to a bowl and add the lemon zest and juice, pomegranate seeds, parsley, coriander and mint. Mix everything together then top with the toasted flaked almonds.

LEMONY QUINOA AND PUFFED MILLET

100g quinoa, soaked for 2 hours
200ml vegetable stock
1 tbsp extra virgin olive oil
Sea salt, to taste

1 unwaxed lemon,
zested and juiced
20g puffed millet
1 bunch of parsley, chopped

Rinse the quinoa until the water runs clear, then drain. Bring the vegetable stock to the boil and add the quinoa. Lower the heat to a simmer and cook for about 12 minutes uncovered until tender. Once cooked, transfer the quinoa to a bowl then stir in the olive oil, salt and the lemon zest and juice.

Chill in the fridge and once cold, stir the puffed millet and chopped parsley through the quinoa. Top with a pinch of lemon zest and fresh parsley.

ROASTED CARROTS, FERMENTED GOOSEBERRIES AND WILD MUSHROOMS

200g carrots
Pinch of salt
50g wild mushrooms
25g fermented gooseberries (see below)
1 tbsp Apple Cider Vinegar Living Dressing (see page 175)
Nasturtium leaves or chervil, to garnish

Preheat the oven to 180°c. Wash the carrots, then top and tail them. Place the carrots into the roasting tin whole, or if they are large, slice them into smaller sticks. Toss with a drizzle of olive oil and a pinch of salt.

Roast the carrots in the preheated oven for 20 to 30 minutes, turning halfway, until soft and coloured. While the carrots are in the oven, sear the mushrooms in a pan on a high heat with a little olive oil and salt until browned, about 2 to 3 minutes. Once the carrots are cooked, leave them to cool slightly, then chop into bite-size chunks or batons.

Toss the carrots in a bowl with the dressing and plate up with the seared mushrooms and fermented gooseberries. Garnish with nasturtium leaves or chervil if desired.

FERMENTED GOOSEBERRIES

200g fresh gooseberries
1 tsp non-iodised salt

Wash the gooseberries then pat them dry. Mix the berries with the salt in a bowl, coating them well without breaking them. Transfer to a Kilner jar making sure to bring all the salt from the bowl. Press the mixture down with a fermenting weight. Ferment the berries at room temperature for about a week. Taste after 5 days, it should be slightly soured, but still have a sweet and fruity aroma. You can also freeze the berries in an airtight container to prevent them from fermenting further.

≋ ⚡ ✿ ♡ ◉ NATURAL · FERMENTED · LIVING FOOD

BABY CARROTS WITH SMOKED ALMOND AND KALE CRUMB

500g baby carrots
200g smoked almonds
200g kale
50g nutritional yeast

2 tbsp extra virgin olive oil
2 cloves of garlic
1 bunch of parsley

Preheat the oven to 160°c. To make the almond and kale crumb, put everything except the carrots into a blender and pulse until the consistency resembles sand. Spread the mixture in an even layer on a baking tray lined with greaseproof paper then bake in the preheated oven until crispy, for around 20 to 30 minutes.

Meanwhile, wash the carrots and trim the tops off. Take the crumb out of the oven when it's finished baking and increase the temperature to 180°c. Place the carrots on a separate lined baking tray and roast in the oven for 20 minutes, until lightly coloured and tender. Lay the carrots on a dish and cover generously in the crumb.

ROASTED CARROTS WITH ORANGE KOMBUCHA DRESSING

500g mixed carrots (purple, white, sandy)
1 tsp extra virgin olive oil
Pinch of sea salt
Orange Kombucha Dressing (page 181)

Preheat the oven to 180°c. Wash the carrots, then top and tail them. Add the carrots whole to a baking tray with a drizzle of olive oil and a pinch of salt, tossing to coat them. Roast in the preheated oven for 20 minutes until soft and coloured. Leave to cool slightly, then chop into bite-size chunks. When you are ready to serve, toss the carrots with the Orange Kombucha Dressing.

CARROT HISPI CABBAGE SLAW WITH SHIO KOJI MAYO

100g carrot
100g hispi cabbage

Shio koji mayo:
2 tsp Dijon mustard
10ml apple cider vinegar
10g shio koji (fermented rice seasoning)
50ml extra virgin olive oil

To serve:
Parsley, chopped
Chives, chopped
Pink radishes, shaved
A squeeze of lemon juice

Wash and peel the carrots, then coarsely grate into a large bowl.
Slice the hispi cabbage thinly and add to the carrots.

For the mayo, combine the mustard, apple cider vinegar and shio koji in a bowl.
Slowly whisk in the olive oil to emulsify the dressing. Add salt to taste.

Gently mix the shio koji mayo through the carrots and cabbage.
Garnish with fresh chopped parsley, chives and shaved pink radishes
then finish with a squeeze of lemon. Enjoy immediately.

KALIBOS AND RAINBOW RADISH SLAW

1 kalibos cabbage
1 bunch of rainbow radishes
100g Biotic Mayo (see page 178)
1 tbsp chives, chopped
1 tbsp parsley, chopped
Pinch of sea salt

Thinly slice the cabbage and radishes. Gently mix all the ingredients together and serve.

     NATURAL · FERMENTED · LIVING FOOD

BIOTIC SLAW

200g white cabbage
100g carrot, grated
50g Biotic Mayo (see page 178)
1 tbsp fresh lemon juice
Pinch of sea salt, to taste
Chives, to garnish

Finely shred the white cabbage using a food processor or large knife. Put the cabbage in a large bowl with the grated carrot. Add the mayo and lemon juice, adding a little water to loosen the mayo if necessary. Toss to evenly coat the cabbage and carrots in the dressing, season to taste, and serve with finely chopped chives scattered on top.

RED CHICORY AND FIG SALAD
WITH FRESH GOAT'S CHEESE AND WALNUT

4 figs
2 heads of red chicory
1-2 tbsp extra virgin olive oil
50g activated walnuts
(see page 18)

50g hard goat's cheese
1 tbsp honey

Slice the figs into quarters and put them into a large bowl. Keep the ends on the chicory so you can slice the leaves lengthways in quarters, then rinse and pat dry. Place in the bowl with the figs and drizzle with the olive oil. Toast the walnuts in a dry heavy-based pan on a medium heat until they gain some colour and begin to release a nutty aroma. Remove from the heat and allow to cool.

Once the toasted walnuts have cooled, toss them with the chicory and figs to coat with the olive oil, then arrange the salad on a serving dish and crumble the goat's cheese on top. Drizzle with a good quality honey and serve.

SIMPLE GRILLED GEM LETTUCE
WITH KOMBUCHA DRESSING

2 gem lettuce hearts
Sea salt
A dash of extra virgin olive oil
50ml Kombucha Reduction Dressing (see page 180)

Wash and halve the gem lettuces lengthways from top to bottom. Season with salt, and leave them to soften in the salt for a few minutes on a plate. Once they've released a bit of water, pour this off, pat dry and place in a large bowl. Lightly dress with olive oil and a pinch more salt and pepper. Heat a grill pan on medium heat, and sear the lettuce, cut side down first. Once there are grill marks on the cut side, turn the lettuce over to grill evenly on the other side. Return the grilled lettuce to the bowl and toss with the kombucha reduction. Serve on a plate and drizzle with any remaining juices.

BELUGA LENTILS

ENERGY · HIGHLY ENERGISING

200g Beluga lentils, soaked for up to 24 hours
400ml water
20g ginger, grated
20g dark miso paste
2 tsp lime juice
Extra virgin olive oil

Rinse and drain the soaked lentils. Bring the water to a boil in a medium saucepan, add the lentils and cook uncovered for 20 minutes, until al dente but cooked through.

Combine the ginger, miso paste, lime juice and olive oil in a large bowl. Once the lentils are done, transfer them to a colander and drain well. Add them to the bowl of dressing while still warm and stir until coated well.

Allow the lentils to sit for a few minutes to absorb the dressing before serving. Alternatively, cool them in the fridge for further flavour infusion and enjoy cold.

Did you Know

Beluga lentils are black lentils that get their name from their resemblance to Beluga caviar. They are low in calories, rich in iron and folate and an excellent source of protein. They are also packed with health-promoting polyphenols that may reduce several heart disease risk factors.

Black Beluga lentils are a good source of both soluble and insoluble fibre. A high fibre diet has been shown to reduce cholesterol and blood pressure, improve digestion, help to lower blood sugar levels, and contribute to a healthy weight. A 70:30 ratio of prebiotics to probiotics is good for preventing potential bloating from generous helpings of fermented foods, especially before we get used to eating larger quantities. At High we soak and activate the lentils then marinate them with immune-boosting ginger.

CLASSIC HUMMUS

Hummus is delicious eaten as a dip with fresh sourdough and your favourite vegetables, or as a high fibre and protein addition to your High Bowl. We have made many different flavours at the café, so the best way to approach this staple is to give you a base recipe and our favourite creative ways to add flavour if desired.

200g dried chickpeas, soaked for 8-12 hours
30g tahini
2 cloves of garlic, peeled and crushed (optional)
40ml extra virgin olive oil, plus extra to finish

40ml lemon juice
1 lemon, zested
1 tbsp sea salt, or more to taste
Pinch of cayenne pepper

To cook the chickpeas, drain and rinse them, then tip into a heavy-based pan. Add enough cold water to cover them by 10cm, bring to the boil then reduce to a simmer and cook for about 1 hour. Once the beans are tender, remove from the heat, add a pinch of salt and allow the beans to cool in the liquid. Drain the cooled chickpeas and put them in a food processor or blender with the tahini, garlic, olive oil, lemon juice and zest, salt, and 2 tablespoons of hot water. Pulse then blend until smooth. Add a little more water to reach your desired consistency. Season with salt, pepper and more lemon juice to taste. Top the hummus with a drizzle of olive oil and a sprinkle of cayenne pepper to serve.

JALAPENO AND AVOCADO

200g Classic Hummus
½ avocado
1 lime, zested

20g fresh jalapeño chillies,
deseeded and finely diced
Fresh coriander, chopped

Blend the hummus base with the avocado and lime zest until smooth, then add the jalapeños and fresh coriander. Pulse for just long enough to combine. Taste to check the seasoning. You may want to add a little juice from the jalapeños to add extra sourness and kick. Top the hummus with slices of jalapeño, lime zest, fresh chopped coriander and olive oil.

PUMPKIN AND CUMIN SEED

200g Classic Hummus
100g pumpkin, peeled and diced
1 tbsp extra virgin olive oil
1 tbsp cumin seeds

1 tsp fennel seeds
30g pumpkin seeds
A squeeze of lemon juice
Salt and pepper, to taste

Preheat the oven to 180°c and line a baking tray with greaseproof paper. Coat the diced pumpkin in the oil then roast in the oven for about 25 minutes, until soft. Heat a heavy-based pan then add the cumin and fennel seeds. Once toasted, remove them from the pan and add the pumpkin seeds to toast until they release a nutty aroma. Once the pumpkin is cooked, blend it with the spices and seeds until smooth. Add the hummus base to your pumpkin puree and blend to combine. Add lemon juice, salt and pepper to taste. Chill before serving and top with a drizzle of olive oil, some fresh chopped coriander, and more toasted pumpkin seeds.

BEETROOT, SESAME AND LABNEH

200g Classic Hummus
1 beetroot, washed
2 tbsp labneh or coconut yoghurt
Salt and pepper, to taste

2 tbsp black and white
sesame seeds, toasted
1 tbsp chives, chopped

Preheat the oven to 180°c. Wrap the beetroot in foil and cook in the oven for 45 minutes until tender. Allow to cool then peel with a knife; the skin should come off easily. Blend the beetroot to a smooth puree then blend again with the hummus base and half the labneh or yoghurt. Season to taste. When you are ready to serve your hummus, stir through the remaining labneh or yoghurt. Top with a drizzle of olive oil, the toasted sesame seeds and freshly chopped chives.

TOMATO CHICKPEA SALAD

50g chickpeas, soaked for 8-12 hours
50g arugula
1 bunch of fresh basil
1 clove of garlic, peeled
2 tbsp extra virgin olive oil

1 lemon, zested and juiced
Sea salt and freshly
ground black pepper
200g cherry tomatoes

To cook the chickpeas, drain and rinse them, then tip into a heavy-based pan.
Add enough cold water to cover them by 10cm, bring to the boil then reduce to
a simmer and cook for about 1 hour. Once the beans are tender, remove from
the heat, add a pinch of salt and allow the beans to cool in the liquid.

For the salad, start by roughly chopping the arugula, basil and garlic. Add them to a small
food processor with the olive oil, lemon juice, half the lemon zest, 1 teaspoon of sea
salt and a good crack of black pepper. Blend well to achieve a smooth green dressing.

Halve the cherry tomatoes and put them into a large bowl with the
drained chickpeas. Stir in the green dressing to coat everything evenly.
Serve the salad cold and garnish with a few whole basil leaves.

SWEET POTATO SAAG ALOO

2 medium sweet potatoes
2 red onions
1 tbsp coconut oil
1½ tbsp apple cider vinegar
2 tbsp madras curry paste

1 tsp sea salt
500g spinach leaves
40g coconut yogurt
1 bunch of coriander, chopped

Peel and chop the sweet potatoes into 5cm cubes. Place them in a saucepan
with enough hot water to cover, and boil for 10 minutes until tender. Peel and
dice the red onions while you heat the coconut oil in a heavy-based pan. Sauté
the onion until translucent, then deglaze the pan with the apple cider vinegar.
Add the curry paste and stir to combine it with the onions, then drain and add
the cooked sweet potatoes. Season with salt. Add the spinach leaves to the
pan and stir for a couple of minutes until they wilt, then remove the pan from
the heat and stir through the coconut yoghurt to form a creamy sauce.
Garnish with the fresh chopped coriander.

    NATURAL • FERMENTED • LIVING FOOD

KALE AND BUTTER BEAN SALAD

100g butter beans,
soaked for 6-8 hours
250g kale
2 tbsp extra virgin olive oil
2 tsp lemon juice

1 tsp sea salt
2 tbsp flaked almonds, toasted
50g pomegranate seeds

To cook the butter beans, drain off the soaking water and rinse them in a colander under a running tap. Put the butter beans in a heavy-based pan. Add enough cold water to cover them by 10cm, bring to the boil then reduce to a simmer and cook for about 1 hour. Once the beans are tender, remove from the heat, add a pinch of salt and allow the beans to cool in the liquid, then drain and rinse them. To make the salad, remove the stalks from the kale then roughly chop or tear the leaves into small pieces. Combine the olive oil, lemon juice and salt then rub this into the kale using your hands. This partially breaks down and softens the kale, making it easier to eat, while thoroughly coating and dressing the leaves. Once the leaves are looking slightly darker and shiny, add the cooked butter beans, toasted flaked almonds and pomegranate seeds to the kale. Stir everything together, add an extra pinch of salt and fresh black pepper to taste, then serve.

SZECHUAN AUBERGINE
WITH MISO AND APPLE CIDER VINEGAR

4 aubergines
100g dark miso paste
100ml apple cider vinegar
100ml maple syrup

2 cloves of garlic
10 Szechuan peppercorns
20g black sesame seeds
A squeeze of lime juice

Preheat the oven to 180°c. Wash the aubergines then cut them into even slices. Lay the rounds on a wire rack and salt on both sides. Let them 'sweat' while preparing the marinade.

Place the miso paste, apple cider vinegar, maple syrup, garlic and peppercorns into a blender and blend until smooth. Pat the aubergine slices dry and lay on a lined baking tray. Brush them with the marinade on both sides and roast in the preheated oven for around 15 minutes until dark and sticky. Serve immediately, garnished with sesame seeds and a squeeze of lime.

NATURAL · FERMENTED · LIVING FOOD

TENDERSTEM BROCCOLI WITH PINE NUTS

200g tenderstem broccoli
20g pine nuts
2 tsp extra virgin olive oil
½ tsp sea salt

Trim off the bottom of the broccoli stems. Toast the pine nuts in a
dry pan on low heat. Stir occasionally until the pine nuts are evenly
golden brown. Remove from the heat and allow to cool.

Lightly oil the broccoli and either cook under the grill or in a hot
pan until it is cooked through and has a nice colour.

Toss the broccoli with the pine nuts, season with salt and eat either hot or
cold. You could try it with our Apple Cider Vinegar Living Dressing (see page
175) and garnish with nutritional yeast as an alternative to salt.

BROCCOLI AND CASHEW PESTO SALAD

1kg broccoli
2 tsp extra virgin olive oil
2 tsp sea salt
50g baby spinach leaves
100g Cashew, Roasted Garlic and Spinach Pesto (see page 152)

Preheat the oven to 200°c. Wash the broccoli and break or cut it into bite-size florets.
Drizzle the broccoli with the olive oil and salt, rolling it around to coat each piece well.
Lay the broccoli flat on a baking tray and roast in the oven for 8 to 9 minutes.
Set aside to cool. Combine it with the spinach then drizzle with pesto to serve.

SEARED COURGETTE
WITH FETA AND KEFIR

4 courgettes or patty pan squash
50ml kefir
50g full-fat Greek yoghurt
50g feta cheese
1 unwaxed lemon, zested and juiced
Sea salt and cracked black pepper
1 bunch of mint, chopped

Cut the courgette or patty pan squash into bite-size chunks. In a hot pan
greased with olive oil, colour every side of the vegetables. Transfer them
to a bowl and allow to cool slightly before mixing with the rest of the
ingredients, using half of the lemon zest and checking the flavour before
seasoning. Serve in a bowl and garnish with the chopped mint.

CASHEW, ROASTED GARLIC
AND SPINACH PESTO

4 large cloves of garlic
200g activated cashew nuts
200ml extra virgin olive oil
100g spinach

50g basil
1 lemon, juiced
2 tsp sea salt
1 tbsp nutritional yeast

Preheat the oven to 160°c. Roast the cloves of garlic in their skins for 8 to 10 minutes until
soft. On the same tray, toast the cashews until golden, about 6 to 8 minutes. Blend the oil,
spinach, basil, roasted garlic, lemon juice and salt until smooth. Add the toasted cashews
and nutritional yeast then pulse until the pesto reaches your desired consistency.

  NATURAL · FERMENTED · LIVING FOOD

TOMATO, SUMAC, FETA
AND PICKLED ONIONS

1 red onion, finely sliced
50ml red wine vinegar
200g heirloom tomatoes, a mix
of colours and varieties
50g feta cheese, diced

1 bunch of parsley, chopped
Pinch of sumac
1 lemon, zested and juiced
Extra virgin Olive oil
Sea salt and black pepper

To make the pickled onions, place your sliced red onion into a bowl. Bring
the red wine vinegar to the boil in a saucepan. Once boiling, pour the vinegar
over the onions, which will soften in the hot liquid. Once the onions have
reached your desired texture, strain off the vinegar and leave to cool.

Slice the tomatoes and add to a bowl with the onions, feta, parsley, sumac, lemon zest and
juice. Drizzle wih olive oil, mix everything and season to taste with salt and black pepper.

OVEN BAKED
SWEET POTATO

2 large sweet potatoes
A drizzle of extra virgin olive oil
A good pinch of sea salt

4 sprigs of rosemary
4 sprigs of thyme
4 cloves of garlic

Preheat the oven to 180°c. Wash and dry the sweet potatoes. Leave the skins on and place
the potatoes on a lined baking tray. Prick them with a fork, drizzle with olive oil, season
with salt, sprinkle with the herbs and tuck the unpeeled garlic cloves underneath.

Depending on the size of your potatoes, roast for about 30 minutes until crisp on
the outside and soft in the center. Cut in half to serve and drizzle with olive oil.

   NATURAL · FERMENTED · LIVING FOOD

CHARRED CORN
WITH PIQUILLO PEPPERS AND KIMCHI SALT

2 corn on the cob
1 tbsp coconut oil
50g preserved piquillo peppers in oil
1 unwaxed lemon, zested and juiced
Pinch of Kimchi Salt (see below)

Preheat a dry frying pan until very hot; the pan should start smoking.

Taking care not to burn yourself, brush the corn cobs with a small
amount of coconut oil and add them to the pan.

Use tongs to roll the corn around the pan to achieve an even colour all over.
Once nicely charred, take out of the pan and use a knife
to cut the sweetcorn kernels off the cob.
Dice the piquillo peppers and reserve the oil. Whisk this with the lemon juice to make a
dressing. Combine everything in a bowl, season with kimchi salt and enjoy hot or cold.

KIMCHI SALT

Drain a jar of kimchi and spread out thinly
on a tray. Place in the oven at 50°c and
dehydrate overnight or for a minimum of 12
hours until the kimchi is light and crispy.

Pulverise the dried kimchi in a blender
and use as an alternative to salt.

PROTEINS

At High we recommend a veg-centric approach and add the protein as a side dish to your spread of salads. Protein is an important nutritional building block that complements your meal. How much you choose to eat depends on your preferences and training goals.

We would recommend an ethically sourced animal protein, such as 'happy chicken' or wild fish.

If you choose not to eat meat, we suggest trying tempeh, a fermented soy bean product.

TEMPEH SATAY

200g organic tempeh
1 tbsp sesame seeds
1 tbsp fresh coriander, chopped

Satay Sauce:
50g peanut butter
2 tbsp Living Hot Sauce
(see page 176)
1 tbsp tamari
1 tbsp maple syrup
1 lime, juiced
1 tbsp sesame oil

Preheat the oven to 180°c. Slice the tempeh into sticks about 2cm thick. Coat lightly with a drizzle of olive oil and sprinkle with the sesame seeds. Lay on a lined baking tray and roast for 15 minutes, turning halfway, to achieve a golden colour all over.

While the tempeh is in the oven, whisk the ingredients for the satay sauce together in a bowl and season to taste. Transfer to a small dipping bowl. Serve the roasted tempeh hot or cold with the satay sauce, garnished with the chopped coriander.

STICKY MISO TEMPEH

200g tempeh
3 tbsp miso
3 tbsp maple syrup
3 tbsp lime juice
½ tbsp sesame seeds

Preheat the oven to 180°c. Slice the tempeh into sticks about 2cm thick. Combine the miso, maple syrup and lime juice in a bowl then brush this glaze onto the tempeh. Lay flat on a lined baking tray and sprinkle with the sesame seeds. Place in the oven to roast for around 15 minutes, checking that the tempeh doesn't burn as the sugar in the coating can catch quickly. Remove from the oven when golden and caramelised. Enjoy the miso tempeh hot or cold.

    NATURAL · FERMENTED · LIVING FOOD

BAKED GREEN TEMPEH FALAFEL

200g tempeh
50g activated walnuts
50g baby spinach
50g onion
4 cloves of garlic
30g ground almonds
1 bunch of fresh coriander,
fresh basil and fresh parsley
4 tbsp filtered water

2 tbsp extra virgin olive oil
2 tbsp ground flax seeds
1 tsp ground cumin
¾ tsp ground coriander
½ tsp baking powder
½ tsp sea salt
½ tsp black pepper
¼ tsp cayenne pepper

Preheat the oven to 180°c. Place all the ingredients in a
food processor and blend to a dough-like mixture.

Use your hands to roll the mixture into 18 approximately 50g
balls, and place these on a lined baking tray. Bake the falafel in
the preheated oven for 15 minutes, turning them over halfway
through the cooking time, until golden. Serve warm or cold.

High Tip

High calcium bioavailability makes tempeh an excellent plant
protein, especially for vegans and vegetarians. It is made from whole
fermented soy beans and filled with fibre which is great for the gut.
Research indicates that tempeh helps to reduce cholesterol and
menopausal symptoms and can promote increased muscle recovery
and bone density. It has high levels of vitamins B5, B6, B3 and B2.

   NATURAL • FERMENTED • LIVING FOOD

CURED SALMON

1 side of high quality salmon, skin on
(let the fishmonger know it will be for curing)
500g rock salt
250g sugar
2 lemons, zested
2 oranges, zested
4 juniper berries
10 fennel seeds

Wash the salmon then pat it dry and lay on
a dish. Put the rock salt, sugar, zest, juniper
berries and fennel seeds into a food processor
or blender. Pulse and blend everything together
until the mixture has a sandy texture.

Pour the cure over the salmon and gently rub
it in to coat the fish. Cover the dish, and place
in the fridge for 6 hours or overnight.

Take the salmon out the fridge, rinse off the cure
and pat dry with a cloth. The cured salmon can be
finely sliced and served raw, poached or baked.

NATURAL • FERMENTED • LIVING FOOD

CHICKEN WITH SALSA VERDE

4 organic chicken breasts
100ml olive oil
½ bunch of parsley
½ bunch of basil
½ bunch of chives
50g green olives

20g capers
2 tsp Dijon mustard
2 chillies
1 clove of garlic
1 unwaxed lemon,
zested and juiced

Preheat the oven to 180°c. Put the chicken breasts on a tray lined with greaseproof paper and into the oven for 25 minutes until cooked through, then let them rest for 10 minutes. For the salsa verde, blend all the remaining ingredients together until smooth. The salsa will keep in the fridge for up to 5 days. Slice the chicken breasts, roll them in the salsa verde and serve.

CHICKEN WITH COCONUT AND LEMON

4 organic chicken breasts
5ml extra virgin olive oil
Pinch of salt
100g coconut yoghurt
1 unwaxed lemon, zested and juiced
20g parsley, chopped
10g mint, chopped

Preheat the oven to 180°c. Roll the chicken in the olive oil and salt. Put the chicken on a tray lined with greaseproof paper and into the oven for 25 minutes until cooked through, then leave to cool. Meanwhile, mix the yoghurt, lemon zest and juice, parsley and mint together. Slice the cooled chicken and coat the pieces in the yoghurt mixture to serve.

CULTURED CORONATION CHICKEN

4 organic chicken breasts
Extra virgin olive oil
Salt and black pepper
100ml kefir
100g yoghurt
A squeeze of lemon juice

Curry paste:
2 onions, roughly chopped
5 cloves of garlic
30g ginger, roughly chopped
2 chillies
2 tbsp tomato puree
20g curry powder

Garnish:
Flaked almonds, toasted
Chillies, finely chopped
Coriander, chopped
Raisins or sultanas (optional)

Preheat the oven to 180°c. Place the onions, garlic, ginger, chillies, tomato puree and curry powder into a food processor and blend into a paste. Heat a drizzle of olive oil in a saucepan and gently cook the curry paste for 2 minutes, stirring constantly. Chill in the fridge.

Meanwhile, place the chicken breasts in a baking dish. Lightly drizzle them with oil and season with salt and black pepper. Place in the preheated oven to cook for 20 to 25 minutes. When pierced with a knife, the juice released from the chicken should be clear. Allow to cool.

Combine your chilled curry paste with the kefir and yoghurt in a large bowl, then season to taste with salt, pepper and lemon juice. Slice the cooled chicken breast into bite-size pieces and add them to the bowl of coronation dressing. Mix well to coat the chicken. Cool in the fridge to infuse the chicken and develop the flavour further. Serve the coronation chicken garnished with toasted flaked almonds, fresh chilli, fresh coriander and raisins or sultanas, if desired.

SPANISH CHICKEN

50g butter beans, soaked for 6-8 hours
50g kidney beans, soaked for 4-12 hours
Olive oil
1 small onion, chopped
2 cloves of garlic, minced
Salt and black pepper
1 tbsp smoked paprika
½ tsp ground cumin
4 organic chicken thighs
200g tomatoes, chopped
1 red pepper, chopped
1 bay leaf
50ml fermented chilli sauce (see page 177)
20g fresh basil, chopped
20g fresh parsley, chopped

Preheat the oven to 180°c. To cook the beans, drain off the soaking water and rinse them in a colander under a running tap. Put the beans in a heavy-based pan. Add enough cold water to cover them by 10cm, bring to the boil then reduce to a simmer and cook for about 1 hour. Once the beans are tender, remove from the heat, add a pinch of salt and allow the beans to cool in the liquid, then drain and rinse them.

Heat a little olive oil in a heavy-based pan with a lid. Sweat the onion with the garlic, salt and pepper until the onions are soft and translucent but not coloured. Now add the paprika and cumin to the pan and cook gently for 2 minutes. Remove the onion and garlic from the pan temporarily, turn up the heat and add a drizzle more olive oil. Sear the chicken thighs until golden all over, then add the tomatoes, red pepper, cooked beans, bay leaf and the onion and garlic. Stir then cover with the lid and cook in the preheated oven for 30 to 40 minutes.

Finish by stirring through the fermented chilli sauce and top with the chopped fresh herbs. Serve hot.

≈ ⚡ 🪷 🌿 👁 **NATURAL · FERMENTED · LIVING FOOD**

GOAT'S CHEESE WITH BEE POLLEN AND ROASTED MUSCAT GRAPES

400g goat's cheese log
60g muscat grapes
1 tsp bee pollen
1½ tbsp Kombucha Reduction (see page 180)

Preheat the oven to 180°c.

Slice the goat's cheese into 2cm thick rounds, remove the grapes from the stalk, and place both on a lined baking tray.

Bake the cheese and grapes in the oven for 8 to 12 minutes until the cheese is golden, and the grapes are coloured but still holding their shape.

Plate the cheese then scatter over the grapes and bee pollen. Add a drizzle of kombucha reduction for a hint of extra sweetness and sourness if desired.

SALAD DRESSINGS
And Toppings

Traditional salad dressings are often full of artificial thickeners, stabilisers and sugar. Our fermented salad dressings are a great way to get more beneficial bacteria into your diet and make your salad so much tastier!

Our toppings are made from activated seeds, adding that extra special crunch to every meal.

NATURAL · FERMENTED · LIVING FOOD

APPLE CIDER VINEGAR LIVING DRESSING

Makes 250ml

130ml extra virgin olive oil
60ml apple cider vinegar
2 tbsp Dijon mustard
50ml filtered water
½ tsp stevia
¼ tsp salt

Add all the ingredients to a blender and blend until combined. Taste and add more salt if needed.

LIVING HOT SAUCE

Makes 500ml

1kg mixed red chillies
20g salt

Remove the woody stems from the chilies. Should you prefer a chunkier sauce, finely slice your chillies and stir through the salt. Alternatively, for a smoother consistency, simply add the chillies and the salt to a blender and pulse then blend to a puree.

Place your salted chilli mixture in a 1.5L Kilner jar and press everything down to ensure there are no air bubbles. Put a fermentation weight on top, and close the lid. Allow to ferment for a week. If you opted for a smoother sauce and wish to process it further, strain your fermented chillies through a sieve to remove the seeds, and puree once again in a blender until silky.

FIVE ALARM CHILLI

60g salt
3L water
5 red bell peppers
1 yellow bell pepper
7 red chillies
2 green chillies
3 Thai bird's eye chillies
3 scorpion chillies (hot)
1 small onion
1 red onion
7 cloves of garlic
1 tbsp mustard seeds
1-2 tsp smoked paprika

In a large saucepan, dissolve the salt in the water to create a brine.
Slice the bell peppers into large chunks, remove the woody stems
from the chilies, peel and quarter the onions and the garlic.

Starting with the smallest ingredients, pack the mustard seeds, garlic, chillies,
onion and peppers into a 4L Kilner jar. Press everything down firmly and
place a fermentation weight on top. Pour in enough brine to almost fill the
jar, making sure the liquid covers the vegetables, and seal with the lid.
Ferment at room temperature for 6 to 8 weeks.

Once fermented, strain the vegetables while reserving the brine.
Place the fermented vegetables and the smoked paprika into a food
processor or blender and puree the mixture into a sauce, adding small
amounts of the brine as you go to reach your desired consistency.

BIOTIC MAYO

2 egg yolks
1 tbsp Dijon mustard
1 tbsp miso paste
1 clove of garlic, crushed (optional)
250ml extra virgin olive oil
2 tbsp apple cider vinegar
¼ tsp salt

Ensure you have all your ingredients accurately weighed and set out ready to use. Whisk together the egg yolks, Dijon mustard, miso paste and garlic (if using) in a large bowl.
Once combined, very slowly stream in the olive oil while whisking thoroughly.
By hand, this will take around 5 minutes, but you can use a electric whisk or blender here too.
The mayonnaise should start to thicken as you reach the end of the oil, and you can start to pour it in faster. Once the texture is thick and resembles mayonnaise, add the apple cider vinegar and salt then whisk briefly to incorporate. Taste and adjust the seasoning as needed.

MISO TAHINI DRESSING

Makes 250ml

120g tahini
120ml filtered water
1½ tbsp maple syrup, or a few drops of stevia
3 tbsp apple cider vinegar
1½ tbsp miso paste
1 tsp salt

Put the tahini, water and maple syrup in a blender to combine. Add the apple cider vinegar, miso paste and salt, and blend on a high speed for about 1 minute until the dressing is fully mixed and smooth.

    NATURAL • FERMENTED • LIVING FOOD

High Tip

One of the most popular 'grab and go' pots we had at the café was our
Biotic Egg Pot: soft-boiled free-range eggs on a bed of spinach
served with our Biotic Mayo and a side of Curried Kraut (see page 53).

This is the perfect gut-boosting savoury snack. You can also turn it
into a high protein meal by adding a base of quinoa and a side of salmon.
With all of its uses, Biotic Mayo is one of our fridge staples. We recommend
elevating any dish or recipe that calls for regular mayonnaise
with this one, not only for its depth of flavour, but also the added
benefits for your gut from the live ingredients. Add some chopped fresh
herbs, or include the clove of crushed garlic for flavour variations.

CELERIAC AND APPLE
KOMBUCHA REMOULADE

This is a variation of the biotic slaw
and can be served with chicken or salmon.

**50ml apple kombucha reduction (apple kombucha
recipe on page 43, reduction method below)**
1 tbsp apple cider vinegar
250ml extra virgin olive oil
1 tbsp wholegrain mustard
¼ whole celeriac, peeled
½ Granny Smith apple, peeled
Salt and black pepper, to taste

Place the apple kombucha reduction and apple cider vinegar into a blender
or food processor, or a jug with a fitting stick blender, and slowly stream in
the oil to emulsify the mixture. Once thickened, stir through the mustard.
Finely slice the celeriac and apple into neat matchsticks. Add
these to your remoulade and season to taste.

KOMBUCHA REDUCTION

500ml kombucha (see page 42)

Place the kombucha in a saucepan on a medium-low heat. Bring to a gentle simmer
and keep your eye on the pan, stirring often. The liquid will stay at the same volume for a while,
then quickly reduce. It should take 15 to 20 minutes until the kombucha cooks down to about 100ml of
thick syrup. Use any flavour of kombucha here, and use the reudction in place of maple syrup
or honey on your favourite sweet breakfast or in dressings.

    NATURAL · FERMENTED · LIVING FOOD

KIMCHI DRESSING

1½ tbsp kimchi brine
1 tbsp apple cider vinegar
1 tbsp hot sauce

1 tsp Dijon Mustard
60ml extra virgin olive oil

Combine the kimchi brine, apple cider vinegar, hot sauce and
mustard in a blender or food processor. Slowly stream in the olive
oil while continuously blending to emulsify the dressing.

Did you Know

Good gut bacteria help break down plant starches and foods that are difficult to digest.
They help the body convert more food into energy by producing vital B vitamins.
More than 400 types live in our digestive system. Beneficial bacteria like acidophilus and
Bifidobacterium help get rid of harmful bacteria; they harmonise the system and create
a conducive environment for a thriving microbiome. The end result is good gut health.

ORANGE KOMBUCHA DRESSING

3 tbsp Orange Kombucha (see page 45)
1 tbsp lemon juice
60ml extra virgin olive oil
Pinch of sea salt

Place the orange kombucha and lemon juice into a blender or food processor,
or a jug with a fitting stick blender, and combine. Don't worry if your mixture
fizzes a bit, just knock out the air before you add the olive oil. Slowly stream in
the oil while blending to emulsify the dressing. Add a pinch of salt to taste.

ACTIVATED TAMARI SEEDS

100g activated pumpkin seeds
100g activated sunflower seeds
100g activated flax seeds
100ml tamari
1 tbsp miso paste
1 tbsp maple syrup (optional)

See page 18 for a guide to activating your seeds. Preheat the oven
to 140°c and line a baking tray with greaseproof paper.

Heat a large, heavy-based pan on a low heat and toast the pumpkin seeds for
roughly 6 minutes, stirring occasionally so they toast all over. Once they are fragrant
and darker in colour, remove from the pan and place in a mixing bowl.

Add the sunflower seeds to the hot pan and toast for about 4 minutes to achieve an
even brown colour. Once toasted, add them to the bowl along with the flax seeds.

In a small saucepan, combine the tamari, miso paste and maple syrup. Bring to the boil to
create a marinade. Remove from the heat after 1 minute and pour over the mixed seeds.

Stir to coat all the seeds in the marinade then pour them onto the lined baking tray. Place
in the preheated oven for 12 minutes, just until dry and crunchy. Watch carefully as they can
burn easily! Allow the seeds to cool, then store in a sealed container in a cool and dry place.

ACTIVATED DUKKAH

200g activated hazelnuts
100g activated almonds
100g activated sunflower seeds
100g activated white sesame seeds
2 tsp cumin seeds
2 tsp coriander seeds
50g smoked paprika
1 tsp sea salt

See page 18 for a guide to activating the nuts. If you like, peel the almonds and hazelnuts to remove their slightly bitter skins.

Preheat the oven to 150°c. Lay the activated hazelnuts and almonds on a baking tray and place in the oven to roast for around 1 hour.

Place a heavy-based pan on a low heat and add the activated sunflower seeds. After 2 to 3 minutes (the seeds should not be totally coloured yet) add the sesame, cumin and coriander seeds and lightly toast until the sesame seeds are golden and fragrant, and the cumin and coriander seeds crackle. Keep stirring to ensure your seeds do not burn and achieve an even colour. Remove from the pan immediately when they are done.

When the nuts are golden brown, remove them from the oven and add to a food processor or blender with the toasted seeds, smoked paprika and sea salt. Pulse into a chunky crumb, then allow the dukkah to cool completely.

SNACKS
Treat Yourself!

We all deserve a little indulgence every now and again, and at High we believe in elevating the nutritional value of everything we eat to its fullest potential. Yes, even a sweet treat can be nourishing!

We try to stay as close to the natural ingredient as possible, using unrefined forms of sweeteners such as honey, coconut sugar, maple syrup or simply the fruit itself such as in our banana bread (see page 199) and allergen-friendly flours like almond and chestnut.

Our sweet treats champion high quality products, which give them their superior nutritional value. We don't believe in cutting corners, especially when it comes to nourishing yourself!

   NATURAL · FERMENTED · LIVING FOOD

LOW CARB BROWNIE

200g unsalted butter
200g dark chocolate
3 organic eggs
80g xylitol
½ tsp vanilla extract
80g almond flour
50g cacao powder
½ tsp sea salt

Walnuts, cacao nibs, chocolate
chunks (optional extras)

Chocolate mousse:
350g dark chocolate
425g boiling water

Preheat the oven to 175°c and line a 27 by 20cm baking tin with greaseproof paper.

Fill one third of a saucepan with boiling water and bring to a simmer. Place a bowl on top, add the butter and chocolate to gently melt over a low heat, stirring occasionally so the bottom doesn't burn. Remove from the heat and leave to cool.

Beat the eggs and xylitol together using an electric whisk for 10 minutes, until thick enough to leave a trail. slowly add the cooled chocolate mixture and the vanilla extract. Gently fold through the almond flour, cacao powder and salt. Fold through any additional nuts, cacao nibs or chocolate chunks. Pour the brownie batter into the lined tin and bake in the preheated oven for 20 to 25 minutes. When baked, leave to cool completely in the tin before turning out and cutting into squares.

In the meantime, make the chocolate mousse. Place chocolate in a bowl and pour the boiling water onto it. Whisk until the chocolate has melted. Place the bowl into another bowl containing iced water. Continue to whisk until the mixture starts to thicken. Remove the bowl of iced water just before the chocolate mixture becomes a mousse consistency, then leave to set in the fridge for 20 minutes before serving the mousse with the brownies.

HIGH'S CHOCOLATE BROWNIE

Makes 10 brownies

200g coconut oil
90g dark chocolate
75g cocoa powder
4 eggs
200g honey
1 tsp vanilla extract
90g chestnut flour
1 tsp sea salt
25g cocoa nibs

Preheat your oven to 150°c. Place an ovenproof dish filled with water
on the bottom shelf to create some humidity inside the oven.

Line a 30 by 30cm baking tray with baking parchment and set aside. Melt the coconut
oil and dark chocolate together in a glass or metal bowl over a saucepan of boiling
water. Sift in the cocoa powder, and combine well to get a smooth consistency.

Using a stand mixer, beat the eggs, honey and vanilla together. Slightly reduce
the speed then gradually add the chestnut flour, one spoonful at a time, and
the salt to the mixer. Turn the speed down once more and slowly stream in the
liquid chocolate mixture. Keep mixing until you have a smooth batter.

Pour the brownie batter into your lined baking tray and spread out evenly using
a spatula or the back of a spoon. Top with the cocoa nibs. Bake in the preheated oven for
35 minutes until the brownies are set, but still have a shiny melted chocolate appearance.

Allow to cool completely before cutting into even squares. Share among loved
ones or colleagues if you are looking for brownie points...no pun intended!

  NATURAL · FERMENTED · LIVING FOOD

CARROT CAKE COOKIES

Makes 10 cookies

135g carrots
60g coconut oil
2½ tbsp maple syrup
80g gluten-free oats
50g activated pecans, roughly chopped (see page 18)
50g sultanas
50g ground almonds
2½ tbsp chia seeds
2½ tbsp ground flax seeds
1 tbsp psyllium husk
1 tsp ground ginger
1 tsp ground cinnamon
1 tsp sea salt

Preheat the oven to 170°c and line a baking tray with greaseproof paper. Coarsley grate the carrots into a mixing bowl. Add the coconut oil and maple syrup. In a separate mixing bowl, combine the remaining ingredients. Add the carrot mixture to the bowl of dry ingredients and mix the two together well. Leave the mixture to sit for 5 to 10 minutes, allowing the psyllium husk, chia and flax seeds to absorb some of the moisture.

Divide the dough into 50g balls and shape into cookies, then lay on the lined baking tray. They will not spread as they bake so no need to space them too far apart. Bake for 12 minutes until lightly golden, then remove from the oven. Once the cookies are cool enough to handle, place them on a wire rack to cool completely.

〰 ⚡ 🪷 💗 👁 NATURAL · FERMENTED · LIVING FOOD

CHOCOLATE CHIP COOKIES

Makes 10 cookies

125g unsalted butter
125g maple syrup
250g ground almonds
30g coconut flour
1 tsp baking powder
1 tsp sea salt
150g dark chocolate chips

Preheat your oven to 170°c and line a baking tray with greaseproof paper.

Place the butter and maple syrup in a saucepan over low heat and gently melt them together. Combine the ground almonds, coconut flour, baking powder and salt in a large mixing bowl, then add the butter and maple syrup. Mix well to combine and form a dough.

Rest the dough in the fridge. This will make it easier to portion, and cool it enough to ensure the chocolate chips won't melt into the dough!

Once cooled, remove the dough from the fridge and stir in the chocolate chips. Divide the dough into ten even balls of roughly 50g, form them into cookie shapes and lay them on the lined baking tray. Don't worry about spacing them too far apart as the cookies will not spread too much as they bake.

Place in the preheated oven to bake for 10 to 12 minutes, until lightly golden brown. Allow to cool and enjoy as fresh as possible!

≋ ⚡ 🪷 🫶 👁 NATURAL · FERMENTED · LIVING FOOD

ALMOND BUTTER COOKIES

Makes 10 cookies

110g pitted dates
110g almond butter
40g coconut oil
110g ground almonds
50g chestnut flour
1 tsp baking powder
Pinch of sea salt
50g 70% high quality dark chocolate

Preheat your oven to 170°c and line a baking tray with greaseproof paper. Place the dates in a saucepan and cover with water. Bring to the boil and simmer for 5 to 10 minutes to soften the dates.

In a separate saucepan, gently melt the almond butter and coconut oil together over a low heat, stirring to combine and prevent them from catching on the bottom of the pan. Place the ground almonds, chestnut flour, baking powder and salt in a large bowl and mix together. Once softened, strain the dates, reserving the liquid. Blend the dates, almond butter, coconut oil and a small amount of the reserved date liquid together until smooth. Fold this mixture into the dry ingredients.

Portion the dough into ten even balls and gently squash each into a cookie shape. Lay them on the lined baking tray without spacing them too far apart, as the cookies will not spread too much as they bake. Bake for 12 minutes in the preheated oven. When the cookies have a slight colour to them, remove from the oven and allow to cool on a wire rack.

Melt the dark chocolate in a heatproof bowl over a saucepan of simmering water. Once the cookies have totally cooled, drizzle them with the melted dark chocolate. Place the cookies in the fridge to set the chocolate before serving.

  NATURAL • FERMENTED • LIVING FOOD

BANANA BREAD

This gluten-free banana bread gets its sweetness only from the ripe bananas within. For a comforting treat, we recommend serving warm or toasting a slice to melt over some kefir butter (see page 33) or a variety of toppings. Try your favourite nut butter, coconut or Greek yoghurt, labneh and a drizzle of honey or kombucha reduction.

Makes 12 servings

8 very ripe bananas
5 eggs
200g buckwheat flour
200g ground almonds
30g activated walnuts (see page 18)
2 tsp ground cinnamon
2 tsp ground ginger
1 tsp baking powder
1 tsp bicarbonate of soda
1 tsp sea salt

Preheat the oven to 150°c and line a 21 by 11cm loaf tin with greaseproof paper.

Place seven of the bananas and all the eggs into a blender and blend until smooth. Combine the remaining ingredients in a large mixing bowl, then stir the egg and banana mixture into the dry ingredients. Pour the batter into your lined loaf tin. Slice the remaining banana and lay the rounds on top with some extra activated walnuts, if desired, to garnish.

Place the banana bread in the preheated oven to bake. After 60 minutes, remove the loaf from the oven and cover with tin foil. Return to the oven to bake for a further 30 minutes, then remove from the oven and place the loaf on a cooling rack to cool.

  NATURAL · FERMENTED · LIVING FOOD

ORANGE KOMBUCHA CHOCOLATE CAKE

Makes 10-12 servings

250g coconut oil
250g coconut sugar
4 eggs
1 large orange, zested and juiced
250g ground almonds
150g polenta
2½ tsp baking powder
A good pinch of sea salt

1L Orange Kombucha (see page 45)
200ml almond milk
150g high quality dark chocolate

Garnish:
Citrus fruits
Cacao nibs

Preheat your oven to 170°c fan and line a round 20cm springform cake tin with greaseproof paper.

Beat the coconut oil and coconut sugar in a stand mixer with a paddle until creamy. If your coconut oil is solid and you need to soften it first, gently melt it in a saucepan on a low heat. Add your eggs one by one to the creamed oil and sugar along with the orange juice. In a separate large mixing bowl, combine the ground almonds, polenta, baking powder, salt and orange zest, then fold the wet mixture into the dry ingredients. Pour the batter into the lined cake tin and bake in the oven for 45 minutes.

While the cake is in the oven, work on the orange kombucha glaze. Pour the orange kombucha into a wide pan and simmer on a low heat for 20 to 30 minutes. Watch out when you start heating it as kombucha has a tendency to bubble over the top of the pan and make a bit of a mess! It will also stay liquid for a while and reduce suddenly, so keep stirring and keep an eye on it. Reduce until it is thick enough to coat the back of a spoon.

Once the cake is cooked and a skewer comes out clean, remove it from the oven and pour over the kombucha glaze. For the ganache, heat the almond milk in a saucepan. Break the chocolate up into small pieces and add to the milk as you whisk to incorporate and melt them together, creating a thick chocolate ganache.

Remove the cake from the tin and place on a serving dish or board. While it is still warm, pour the ganache onto the cake and spread out evenly with a palette knife. Garnish with slices of orange or grapefruit and cacao nibs. Place the whole cake in the fridge and allow the ganache to set before serving.

HIGH'S 'BOUNTY' BAR

Makes 10 bars

160g coconut oil
200g desiccated coconut
2 tbsp coconut milk
1½ tbsp maple syrup
Pinch of salt
100g dark chocolate
50g toasted coconut chips

Line a baking tray with greaseproof paper and set aside.
Gently melt the coconut oil in a saucepan over a low heat.

Place the desiccated coconut, coconut milk, maple syrup and salt in a large
bowl. Once the coconut oil has melted, add it to the bowl and mix well.

Divide the mixture into ten approximately 40g pieces, then form each
piece into a rectangular bar with your hands. Place the bars on the lined
baking tray and place in the freezer for 3 to 4 hours until solid.

When you are ready to coat your frozen coconut bars, break up
the chocolate into small pieces and place in a glass or metal
bowl over a pan of simmering water to melt gently.

One by one, dip the bars into the melted chocolate to coat them evenly. Return
them to the lined baking tray and top with the toasted coconut flakes. Once all
the bars are coated and topped, place the tray in the fridge to set the chocolate.

  NATURAL · FERMENTED · LIVING FOOD

OMEGA FIX SEED BAR

90g rice malt syrup, or 10g stevia
30g cocoa butter
1 tbsp coconut oil
55g tahini
40g activated sunflower seeds (see page 18)
40g activated pumpkin seeds (see page 18)
30g puffed millet, or a puffed ancient grain of your choice
2 tbsp flax seeds
2 tbsp shelled hemp hearts
1 tbsp sesame seeds
1 tsp ground cinnamon

Line a 33 by 23cm tray, tin or dish with greaseproof paper.

Bring a saucepan of water to a simmer and place a heatproof bowl containing the rice malt syrup, cocoa butter and coconut oil on top. Melt and combine them over the simmering water, then remove the bowl from the saucepan and stir in the tahini.

Place the activated sunflower and pumpkin seeds, puffed millet, flax seeds, hemp hearts, sesame seeds and cinnamon in a large mixing bowl. Pour the wet mixture into the dry ingredients, stirring until everything is thoroughly coated and well combined.

Pour the mixture into your lined tray, smooth it out into an even layer then lightly press it down with the back of a spoon to flatten the surface.

Place the tray in the fridge to set for at least 2 hours. Once completely hardened, cut into bars or squares.

  NATURAL · FERMENTED · LIVING FOOD

SPICED ORANGE AND COCOA ENERGY BALLS

Makes 15 balls

135g activated almonds (see page 18)
60g activated hazelnuts (see page 18)
200g pitted dates
100g coconut oil
135g ground flax seeds
100g desiccated coconut
30g cocoa powder, plus extra to coat
1 orange, zested and juiced
1 tbsp ground ginger
2 tsp ground cinnamon
1 tsp ground cardamom
1 tsp pink Himalayan salt
1 tsp vanilla extract

Place the almonds and hazelnuts in a food processor and pulse until fine and sandy. Empty the crumb into a bowl and place the dates and coconut oil into the food processor.

Blend together to a smooth paste, then add the crumb and all the remaining ingredients to the food processor. Blend to form a smooth dough.

Sieve some extra cocoa powder into a bowl or onto a plate. Divide the dough into 15 approximately 50g portions and roll into balls, then roll in the cocoa powder.

Place the energy balls in the fridge to set for 1 hour.

NATURAL · FERMENTED · LIVING FOOD

ACTIVATED TRAIL MIX

Makes 10 servings

75g activated almonds
75g activated hazelnuts
75g activated walnuts
75g activated pecans
75g raisins

75g high quality dark
chocolate drops
50g cocoa nibs

See page 18 for a guide to activating the nuts. If you like, peel the almonds and hazelnuts to remove their slightly bitter skins. Simply combine all the ingredients together in a large bowl. Store in a large Kilner jar for snacking or add to your breakfast for an extra energy-boosting crunch.

MISO-TAMARI NUTS

Makes 10 servings

125g activated almonds
125g activated hazelnuts
125g activated walnuts
125g activated pecans

2 tbsp miso paste
2 tbsp tamari
1½ tbsp maple syrup

See page 18 for a guide to activating the nuts. If you like, peel the almonds and hazelnuts to remove their slightly bitter skins. Preheat the oven to 100°c and line a baking tray with greaseproof paper.

Place the miso paste, tamari and maple syrup in a saucepan and gradually bring to a low boil. Once boiling, turn down the heat and simmer for 2 to 3 minutes while whisking. In a large mixing bowl, combine the nuts. Pour over the hot miso mixture and stir to ensure all the nuts are evenly coated, before spreading them out on the lined baking tray.

Place in the preheated oven for 1 hour until the nuts dry out and become crisp. Check on them after 30 minutes, if they get too dark in colour they will taste burnt. Remove from the oven and leave out to cool. Once completely cooled, break apart and store in an airtight container for up to 4 weeks, or divide into ten 50g snack pack portions.

COCONUT VANILLA
ICE CREAM

Makes 7 servings, or ice lollies

650ml full-fat coconut milk
2 tbsp maple syrup
2 tsp vanilla extract
Pinch of sea salt

Place your ice cream churning bowl in the freezer at least 1 day in advance so it is ice cold when you are ready to churn your ice cream.

Place the coconut milk, maple syrup, vanilla extract and sea salt into a blender and blend on a high speed for 2 minutes until smooth. Transfer the mixture directly to the chilled ice cream churning bowl and churn for about 45 minutes. Once a smooth ice cream consistency is reached, transfer the ice cream to a large freezer-safe container and use a spoon to smooth the top. Cover and freeze until firm.

Before serving, remove the ice cream from the freezer and let it sit at room temperature for 5 minutes to soften up. Using a hot ice cream scoop also helps to form perfect balls when scooping!

To make ice lollies, omit the steps calling for an ice cream churner, and simply pour your ice cream mixture into ice lolly moulds then place in the freezer overnight.

   NATURAL · FERMENTED · LIVING FOOD

NUT BUTTER, BANANA
AND KEFIR ICE CREAM

Makes 6 servings, or 6 ice lollies

300ml kefir
250ml almond milk, or any other plant milk
2 bananas, peeled
50g almond or peanut butter
2 tbsp maple syrup
1 tsp lemon juice
1 tsp sea salt

Place your ice cream churning bowl in the freezer at least 1 day in advance so it is ice cold when you are ready to churn your ice cream.

To make your ice cream, place all the ingredients in a high speed blender or a food processor and blend until smooth.

Transfer the mixture directly to the chilled ice cream churning bowl and churn for about 45 minutes. Once a smooth ice cream consistency is reached, transfer the ice cream to a large freezer-safe container and use a spoon to smooth the top. Cover and freeze until firm.

Before serving, remove the ice cream from the freezer and let it sit at room temperature for 5 minutes to soften up. Using a hot ice cream scoop also helps to form perfect balls when scooping!

To make ice lollies, omit the steps calling for an ice cream churner, and simply pour your ice cream mixture into ice lolly moulds then place in the freezer overnight.

   NATURAL · FERMENTED · LIVING FOOD

RASPBERRY KOMBUCHA SORBET

Makes 6 servings, or 6 ice lollies

500ml kombucha
100g fresh raspberries
2 tbsp maple syrup (optional)

Place your ice cream churning bowl in the freezer at least 1 day in advance
so it is ice cold when you are ready to churn your ice cream.

To make your sorbet, place 100ml of the kombucha into a blender with all the raspberries
and maple syrup. Start blending slowly, as initially the kombucha may fizz up. Ensure
there is a tiny gap for gas to escape. Increase the speed and blend on high for 2 minutes
until smooth. Once you have a smooth puree, stir in the rest of the kombucha. This
way you may maintain some of the kombucha's fizziness. If you prefer a smoother
sorbet, blend all of the kombucha with the maple and raspberries which should
knock out the air (definitely making sure you have a way for the gas to escape!).

Add the mixture directly to the chilled ice cream bowl and churn for about
45 minutes until it's starting to look set, then transfer to a large freezer-safe
container and use a spoon to smooth the top. Cover and freeze until firm.

Before serving, remove the sorbet from the freezer and let it sit at
room temperature for 5 minutes to soften up. Using a hot ice cream
scoop also helps to form perfect balls when scooping!

To make ice lollies, omit the steps calling for an ice cream churner, and simply pour
your sorbet mixture into ice lolly moulds then place in the freezer overnight.

SEASONAL SPREADS

Spring.
Summer.
Autumn.
Winter.

Buying local produce that is in season and grown in good quality soil ensures that we eat the nutrients required for our bodies at different times of the year. Fermenting vegetables and fruit that are harvested in the summer or autumn provides us with vitamins and minerals over the winter months.

We advise looking out for 'happy' animal protein: organic, free-range and pastured animal products are best.

SPRING

Plants: collard greens, spring greens, edible flowers, kale, monk's beard, nettles, peas, radishes, rhubarb, wild garlic, asparagus, broccoli, Jersey Royal potatoes, lettuce and salad leaves, purple sprouting broccoli, rocket, samphire, spinach, spring onions, watercress, wild nettles, basil, chives, dill and sorrel.

Protein: lamb, wood pigeon, cockles, crab, langoustine, lobster, plaice, prawns, salmon, sea trout and shrimp.

CHARRED BABY GEM LETTUCE
WITH SUNFLOWER SEED CRUMB

50g activated sunflower seeds (see page 18)
Pinch of salt or 2 tbsp nutritional yeast flakes, to taste
4 baby gem lettuces
1 tbsp extra virgin olive oil

Lightly chop and toast the sunflower seeds, then add salt or mix them
with the yeast flakes. Cut the baby gems in half and place them cut side
down in a frying pan on a medium heat with the olive oil.

Cook for 2 to 3 minutes until golden in colour. You could also put the baby gems under
the grill in a preheated oven at 200°c for about 5 to 7 minutes. Remove from the pan,
coat generously with the sunflower crumbs and serve. This dish is best enjoyed hot.

MINTED ASPARAGUS
WITH FRESH PEAS, KEFIR AND CURDS

200g fresh peas, blanched
10 trimmed green asparagus stems
1 tsp extra virgin olive oil
100g goat's curd
50g kefir

1 tsp salt
½ lemon, zested and juiced
2 tbsp fresh mint, chopped
1 tbsp fresh chives, chopped

Pop the peas from the pods into a bowl. Thinly slice the asparagus with a mandoline
(or a sharp knife) and toss in a little olive oil. In a separate bowl, mix the goat's
curd with the kefir then season with the salt, lemon zest and lemon juice.

Fold the peas and asparagus into the kefir and goat's curd mixture.
Garnish with the chopped mint and chives.

WARM MILLET SALAD
WITH FENNEL AND ORANGE

---

1 bulb of fennel
2 oranges, segmented
2 tbsp apple cider vinegar
200g millet
400ml water
Pinch of salt
1 tbsp coconut oil
1 tbsp extra virgin olive oil
2 pink radishes, sliced
1 tbsp fresh dill, chopped
1 tbsp fresh chives, chopped

Pick off the fennel tops and save them for later. Shave the bulb of fennel thinly on a mandoline and toss with the orange segments and apple cider vinegar in a mixing bowl, then leave to one side.

In a large dry saucepan, toast the raw millet over a medium heat for 4 to 5 minutes or until it turns a rich golden brown and the grains become fragrant. Add the water and salt to the pan, give the millet a good stir, increase the heat and bring the mixture to the boil. Lower the heat to a simmer, drop in the coconut oil and cover the pan. Simmer until the grains absorb most of the water, about 15 minutes, then remove the pan from the heat and leave the millet to stand, covered, for 10 minutes. Fluff the millet and season with olive oil and salt.

Top the millet with the sliced radishes, chopped dill and chives, the orange and fennel mixture and finally the fennel tops. Drizzle over all the juice left in the bowl.

You could also try this recipe with blood oranges for a delicious twist on a refreshing salad.

  NATURAL · FERMENTED · LIVING FOOD

SADDLE OF EASTER LAMB
WITH WILD GARLIC, CAPER BERRIES,
CAULIFLOWER PUREE AND MISO BROTH

1 shoulder end saddle
of lamb, bone-in

500g lamb bones (talk
to your butcher)

500g bone broth (see page 118)

1 cauliflower

15g extra virgin olive oil

Pinch of salt

15g dark miso

1 bunch of wild garlic

Caper berries, to garnish

Preheat the oven to 180°c and take the saddle of lamb out of the fridge so it sits
at room temperature for a couple of hours before cooking. Roast the lamb bones
in the oven for about 1 hour until golden brown. Pour the bone broth into a large
saucepan, heat until almost boiling then carefully add the roasted lamb bones and
gently simmer the broth for 2 hours, skimming off the fat as it rises to the top.

In the meantime, grate the cauliflower down to the stem and discard the stem. Sweat the
grated cauliflower in the olive oil on a gentle heat until soft but not coloured. Blend the
cauliflower into a puree with a small amount of water and a pinch of salt until smooth.

Strain the lamb broth, then reduce until it coats the back of a spoon. Finish
by stirring in the miso. Bring a pan of salted water to the boil. Rinse the wild
garlic and trim off any fibrous stems, then blanch the leaves in the boiling
water for 10 to 15 seconds. Remove with a slotted spoon and plunge into
some iced water. Drain the wild garlic and pat dry with kitchen paper.

Season the saddle of lamb with salt and place it fat side down in a cold frying pan on
a medium heat. As the fat renders, pour it out of the pan and discard. When the outer
layer of fat is golden brown and crispy, place the lamb on a roasting tray and cook in the
preheated oven for 14 minutes. Rest the lamb for at least 10 minutes before serving.

Carve the lamb and plate with the cauliflower puree, blanched wild
garlic and caper berries. Serve the miso broth on the side.

GRILLED SWEET PEPPERS
WITH TOASTED PINE NUTS AND LEMON

4 corno di toro peppers, or any sweet pepper
4 tbsp extra virgin olive oil
1 tsp salt
1 unwaxed lemon, zested and juiced
100g pine nuts, toasted

Heat griddle pan until it is smoking hot and grill the peppers without oil.
You are looking for a nice char and for the peppers to soften and sweeten.

They are done when you can easily pull the top and seeds out in one.
In a small mixing bowl, whisk the olive oil, salt, lemon zest and lemon juice together.

Pour the lemon dressing over the charred peppers and generously coat
them in the toasted pine nuts. This dish is best served hot.

KALE AND CHARD SALAD
WITH KOMBUCHA DRESSING

100g kale
100g rainbow chard
2 tbsp kombucha reduction (see page 180)
2 tbsp extra virgin olive oil
¼ tsp salt

Remove the stems from the kale and chard by cutting them lengthways along either side of
the stem. Wash and dry all the leaves in a salad spinner. In a small mixing bowl, emulsify the
kombucha, oil and salt by whisking them together. Dress the leaves and serve in a bowl.

BRITISH QUINOA
WITH WILD GARLIC OIL
AND FERMENTED RED ONIONS

Quinoa:
200g British quinoa, soaked
400ml filtered water
1 tsp salt

Wild garlic oil:
75g wild garlic
110g extra virgin olive oil
½ tsp salt

Fermented red onions
(takes 7-14 days):
2 red onions, finely sliced
2 tsp salt
300ml water

Rinse the quinoa under cool running water and add to the filtered
water in a saucepan over a medium heat. Bring to the boil and lower
the heat, season with salt and simmer for 20 minutes.

Blend the wild garlic, olive oil and salt together until the mixture splits. Strain
the liquid through a sieve into a bowl or jar and store the oil in the fridge.

Pack the sliced red onions firmly into a 500ml glass Kilner jar. Dissolve the salt in the
water, then pour the brine over the onions, leaving 2.5cm between the top of the
jar and the surface of the brine. Use a weight to keep the onions under the brine,
if necessary. Let them sit at room temperature on the counter for 7 to 14 days.

Combine 50g of the garlic oil with all the cooked quinoa in a bowl. Stir
to coat the grains and then season with salt. Garnish with 1 tablespoon
of the fermented onions and some raw wild garlic leaves to serve.

    NATURAL · FERMENTED · LIVING FOOD

CHARGRILLED GURNARD
WITH CAPERS AND PRESERVED LEMONS

2 gurnard fillets
1 tsp extra virgin olive oil
1 tsp salt
150g baby leaf salad
1 tbsp fresh chervil, chopped
1 tbsp capers
1 tbsp preserved lemon, flesh removed, skin sliced
Edible flowers for decoration (optional)

Vinaigrette:
2 tbsp liquid from the preserved lemons
4 tbsp extra virgin olive oil
½ unwaxed lemon, zested and juiced

Preheat a griddle pan until it is smoking hot. Whisk the ingredients for the vinaigrette together and set aside. Apply the olive oil to the fish and season with salt. Lay the gurnard into the hot griddle pan to cook for about 3 minutes. Turn the fillets halfway through this time to achieve the same colour and griddle marks on both sides.

When the fish is cooked, remove from the pan and rest for 1 minute before slicing into triangles.

Then dress the baby leaf salad with the vinaigrette and place into a serving bowl. Place the fish on the leaves and top with the chervil, capers and sliced preserved lemon.

Decorate with edible flowers if using.
If chervil is not available, you can also use chopped parsley or tarragon here.

POACHED ASPARAGUS
IN ELDERFLOWER KOMBUCHA

Elderflower kombucha
(takes about 1 week):
500ml neutral tea kombucha
200g elderflowers

1 bunch of trimmed
green asparagus
2 tbsp butter
1 tsp salt
100ml elderflower kombucha

Steep the elderflowers in the kombucha for about 1 week; this will just get better with time. When your elderflower kombucha is ready, put a pan with a tight fitting lid on a low heat. Place the asparagus into the pan in a single layer, add the butter and salt, then pour in just enough elderflower kombucha to half cover the asparagus. Cook with the lid on for 3 minutes until they are tender.
Plate the asparagus and enjoy hot.

BUTTERED CARROTS
WITH THEIR TOPS AND CHERVIL

500g baby carrots
20g butter
2 handfuls of carrot tops
2 handfuls of chervil
1 tsp salt

Wash the carrots and carrot tops. Melt the butter in a saucepan, add the carrots, season with salt and cover with a lid. On low heat, gently cook the carrots for about 8 minutes until tender. Add the chervil and carrot tops to the pan at the last minute to gently wilt them.
Transfer to a bowl and serve hot.

SAN MARZANO TOMATO AND CHICORY WITH FERMENTED CHERRY TOMATOES

300g (about 4) San Marzano tomatoes
50g fermented tomatoes (see below)
1 head of chicory
1 tbsp extra virgin olive oil
1 tbsp fermented tomato brine
1 tbsp fresh chervil, chopped
Salt and pepper, to taste

Cut the San Marzano tomatoes into quarters and mix with the fermented tomatoes. Cut the base off the chicory, then separate the leaves and assemble them in a serving bowl with the tomatoes. Make the dressing by mixing the olive oil and fermented tomato brine together. Season to taste, then pour the dressing over the chicory and tomatoes. Garnish with the fresh chervil to serve.

Fermented tomatoes:
20g salt
600ml filtered water
500g cherry tomatoes
4 cloves of garlic
½ bunch of basil

Prepare the brine by dissolving the salt in the filtered water. Prick each cherry tomato a few times. Pack the garlic and basil into a 1L Kilner jar, folllowed by the tomatoes and the brine. Make sure the tomatoes are covered but leave a 2.5cm gap between the rim of the jar and the surface of the liquid. Place a weight on top to keep everything submerged. Seal the jar with a tight lid and ferment for 5 to 7 days at room temperature. After this fermentation period, store the jar in the fridge.

STUFFED COURGETTE FLOWERS
WITH ALMONDS, KALE AND MUSHROOMS

500g activated almonds, toasted (see page 18)
50g purple kale, chopped
50g mushrooms of your choice, finely chopped
2 tbsp water
1 tsp salt
4 courgette flowers

Reserve 100g of the almonds for later. Put the remaining
400g into a blender with the water and blend until the
mixture splits. Strain the oil off and reserve it.

In a bowl, mix the almond pulp with the chopped kale
and mushrooms. Whisk the almond oil into the mixture,
then season with salt and place in a piping bag.

Cut a 1cm hole in the piping bag and, working gently and
carefully, fill the petals of the courgette flowers with the mix.

Set up a bamboo steamer lined with greaseproof paper in a wok
or large pan and heat until steam starts to appear. Steam the
stuffed courgette flowers lightly for 2 to 3 minutes. Cover the plate
with the reserved almonds and place the flowers on top.

SUMMER

Plants: beans (broad, runner, yellow, green, purple), beetroot, blackcurrant leaves, borage flowers, hispi cabbage, baby carrots, chard, courgette, cucumber, kohlrabi, baby leeks, mustard, dandelion, patty pan squash, tomatoes, samphire, asparagus, aubergines, broccoli, chillies, fennel, garlic, lettuce and salad leaves, mangetout, new potatoes, onions, pak choi, peas, radishes, rocket, spinach, spring onions, turnips, wild nettles, apricots, bilberries, blueberries, cherries, greengages, kiwi fruit, peaches, strawberries, basil, chervil, chives, coriander, dill, elderflowers, oregano, mint, nasturtium, parsley, rosemary, sage, sorrel, tarragon and thyme.

Protein: lamb, venison, beef, chicken, rabbit, wood pigeon, cod, coley, crab, haddock, halibut, herring, langoustine, plaice, pollack, prawns, salmon, sardines, scallops, sea bream, sea trout, shrimp, squid, whelks and whitebait.

   NATURAL • FERMENTED • LIVING FOOD

FERMENTED RADISHES WITH EDAMAME AND CORIANDER

Fermented radishes:
2 tsp salt
300ml water
200g daikon radishes

250g edamame beans
2 tbsp fresh coriander, chopped
1 tbsp extra virgin olive oil
1 bunch of pink radishes

To make the fermented radishes, prepare the brine by dissolving the salt in the water. Wash the radishes well and remove the tops and tails. Cut small radishes into quarters and larger ones into sixths. Pack the radishes into a 500ml Kilner jar and cover with the brine, leaving about 2.5cm of space before the rim of the jar. If necessary, press the radishes down with a weight to keep them submerged. Seal the jar with a tight lid and ferment for 7 days at room temperature.

Cook the edamame beans in salt water until tender. Once the radishes are fermented to your taste, mix them with the beans, coriander and olive oil in a bowl. Serve cold, garnished with thinly sliced raw pink radishes.

CHARRED HISPI CABBAGE WITH KIMCHI GLAZE

200ml kimchi brine
1 tsp maple syrup
1 hispi cabbage
1 tsp salt

Reduce the kimchi brine with the maple syrup in a pan over a low heat until a syrupy consistency is achieved. Meanwhile, cut the cabbage into quarters and season with the salt.

Place the cabbage quarters in a hot pan on a medium heat to colour all sides evenly. Once cooked, remove the core and fold all the leaves into a bowl. Cover the cabbage in the kimchi glaze and enjoy hot.

QUINOA TABBOULEH
WITH POMEGRANATE

200g quinoa
400g water
1 tsp salt
1 bunch of mint
1 bunch of parsley
1 pomegranate
1 unwaxed lemon, zested and juiced
1 tbsp extra virgin olive oil
Salt and pepper, to taste

Rinse the quinoa until the liquid runs clear then drain.
Bring the water to the boil with the salt in a saucepan,
then simmer the quinoa for 20 minutes.

While the quinoa is cooling, chop the parsley and mint, get
the seeds out of the pomegranate then combine the herbs,
pomegranate seeds, lemon zest and juice with the quinoa.

Drizzle in the rapeseed oil and taste the tabbouleh, then
adjust the seasoning with salt and pepper before serving.

ROASTED CHICKEN
WITH LEMON AND THYME

Brine:
1L water
35g salt
6 juniper berries
2 bay leaves
2 sprigs of thyme
1 star anise
1 clove of garlic
1 unwaxed orange,
zested and juiced

1 unwaxed lemon,
zested and juiced

Chicken:
1 whole chicken
500ml chicken bone broth
1 lemon, halved
1 sprig of thyme

Combine all the ingredients for the brine and mix well. Place the chicken into the brine and keep in the fridge for 8 to 12 hours.

The next day, remove the chicken from the brine and pat dry. Preheat the oven to 180°c.

In a deep saucepan, reduce the bone broth to the consistency of gravy then set aside. Meanwhile, stuff the chicken with the lemon halves and a large sprig of thyme.

Roast the chicken in the preheated oven on a rack for 25 minutes. Take the chicken out and turn the temperature up to 220°c. Keep the chicken resting out of the oven for about 10 minutes to allow the oven to get up to temperature. When the oven is hot, put the chicken back in and cook for around 25 minutes until the skin is golden brown and crispy.

Allow the cooked chicken to rest again for 20 minutes. Once rested, carve the roast chicken and serve with lots of the reduced bone broth gravy.

SPICY BROWN RICE

200g brown rice
300ml water
50g coconut oil
50ml Living Hot Sauce
(see page 176)
50ml lime juice

1 tbsp fresh coriander, chopped
1 tbsp fresh mint, chopped
1 tbsp spring onions, chopped

Rinse the rice until the water runs clear, then place into a saucepan
with a tight fitting lid and add the water and coconut oil.

Bring to a rolling boil then reduce to a gentle simmer. Cook uncovered
for 30 minutes, then turn off the heat, add the chilli sauce and lime
juice and stir to combine well. Place the lid on firmly and leave
for at least 15 minutes for the rice to soak up the flavours.

Stir in the chopped coriander, mint and spring onions when ready to serve.

   NATURAL · FERMENTED · LIVING FOOD

BUTTERED RUNNER BEANS AND GIROLLES WITH ACTIVATED HAZELNUTS

10 runner beans
½ white onion
1 clove of garlic
1 tsp butter

100g wild mushrooms,
such as girolles
2 tbsp activated hazelnuts
1 tsp celery salt

Trim the runner beans and run a peeler down the side to remove
the string, then cut each bean into eight pieces.

Bring a large pan of water with a pinch of salt to the boil, add the beans and bring
back to the boil, cook for 2-3 minutes until tender, then drain and set aside.

In a frying pan, sweat the onion and the garlic in the butter, then turn up the heat,
add the mushrooms and cook for 2 minutes until they have coloured. When the
mushrooms are almost cooked, add the hazelnuts and the beans to the pan.
Season with the celery salt and enjoy hot.

BABY LEAF AND BASIL SALAD WITH FERMENTED TOMATOES

1 tsp butter
1 tsp maple syrup
1 slice of goat's cheese
500g baby leaf salad
 2 tbsp grated beetroot

2 tbsp grated carrot
1 tbsp fresh basil, chopped
1 tbsp extra virgin olive oil
6 fermented tomatoes

Melt the butter, add the maple syrup and briefly fry the goat's cheese to caramelise
both sides. Combine the baby leaf salad with the grated beetroot and carrot,
fresh basil and olive oil, then add the fermented tomatoes (see page 233) and
top with the caramelised goat's cheese. A simple pleasure with a twist!

BREAM FILLET
WITH KOMBUCHA AND BROWN BUTTER

1 tbsp extra virgin olive oil
2 small bream fillets (skin on)
50g butter, chilled and diced
200g kombucha
1 lemon, sliced
1 tbsp fresh parsley, chopped
1 tbsp fresh dill, chopped
1 tsp salt
Freshly ground black pepper, to taste

Preheat a non-stick pan over a medium heat. Lightly oil the pan,
add the fish skin side down and gently crisp the skin while applying
some pressure to the top of the fillets to keep the skin flat.

Once the skin is crispy, take the fish out of the pan, add most of the butter
and keep it moving in the pan until it becomes nutty and caramelised.

Put the fish back in the pan, flesh side down in the butter. Once the fish is lightly
cooked, transfer it to a warm plate and add the kombucha to deglaze the pan and
reduce. Whisk in the remaining cold butter to emulsify it with the reduction.

Serve the fish hot covered with the kombucha butter sauce, slices of lemon
and chopped herbs. Season to taste with salt and black pepper.

NATURAL • FERMENTED • LIVING FOOD

GRILLED ROMAINE LETTUCE
WITH CUCUMBER, MINT AND YOGHURT

1 cucumber
1 clove of garlic (optional)
1 bunch of mint
1 tsp lemon zest
1 tsp salt

3 tbsp Greek yoghurt
1 romaine lettuce
1 tsp extra virgin olive oil
Freshly ground black
pepper, to taste

Wash the cucumber, then use a peeler to make long cucumber ribbons. Mince
the garlic if using, and finely chop the mint. Mix the cucumber ribbons, minced
garlic, chopped mint, lemon zest and salt with the yoghurt and set aside.

Cut the romaine lettuce into quarters lengthways. Season the lettuce with salt and olive oil. In
a pan on a high heat, colour the lettuce on all sides for around 4 minutes until golden brown.
Cut the quarters in half and dress them with the cucumber and mint yoghurt.
Season with black pepper to taste then serve in a decorative bowl.

SEARED COURGETTES
WITH LEMON AND MINT YOGHURT

4 courgettes
1 bunch of mint, chopped
2 tbsp kefir
2 tbsp yoghurt
1 tsp unwaxed lemon zest

1 tsp salt
Chilli flakes
Pink pepper

Cut the courgettes into bite-size chunks. In a pan on a medium heat, colour the courgettes
on all sides for around 4 minutes. Transfer them to a bowl and leave to cool slightly.

In a mixing bowl, combine the chopped mint, kefir, yoghurt, lemon zest and salt.
Fold the seared courgettes into the yoghurt mixture. Garnish with a few mint
leaves and sprinkle with chilli flakes and pink pepper to taste before serving.

If patty pans (those little flying saucer shaped squashes) are available at
your market, they are a great alternative to courgettes for this recipe.

NATURAL · FERMENTED · LIVING FOOD

GRILLED AUBERGINE
WITH BURNT LIME AND POMEGRANATE

2 aubergines
1 tbsp extra virgin olive oil
1 tsp salt and black pepper
2 limes, halved
1 pomegranate

Cut the aubergines into 1cm thick strips, lightly brush with
olive oil and season with salt and pepper.

Heat a griddle pan over a high heat then cook the aubergine for around 2 minutes
on each side until they have a charred griddle pattern. Once cooked, remove
from the pan. Place the limes cut side down on the hot griddle to brown.

Plate the aubergines, sprinkle the pomegranate seeds over the top and
decorate with the limes on the side, for squeezing the juice over.

  NATURAL · FERMENTED · LIVING FOOD

TEMPEH
WITH SALSA VERDE

Salsa verde:
70ml extra
virgin olive oil
½ bunch of parsley
½ bunch of basil
½ bunch of chives
2 tbsp capers
30g green olives
1 clove of garlic
1 green chilli
2 tsp Dijon mustard

1 lemon, zested
and juiced
250g tempeh
Extra virgin olive oil
Sea salt

Preheat the oven to 180°c. Cut the tempeh into cubes and coat lightly
with a drizzle of olive oil and pinch of salt. Place on a lined baking tray
to roast in the oven for around 15 minutes until golden brown.

Blend the ingredients for the salsa verde together in a food
processor or blender until they resemble pesto.

Place the roasted tempeh in a large bowl and pour over the salsa verde
while the tempeh is still hot. Stir to combine, then allow the tempeh to soak
up some of the flavour by resting it for 10 minutes or until you are ready to
eat. Place in the fridge and serve cold for a deeper flavour infusion.

AUTUMN

Plants: almonds, chestnuts, chives, cob nuts, hazelnuts, walnuts, purple sprouting broccoli, brussels sprout tops, kalibos cabbage, romanesco, celery, purple kale, mushrooms, pumpkin, salsify, squash, onion, turnip, parsley, rosemary, sage, sorrel and thyme.

Protein: beef, lamb, duck, goose, grouse, guinea fowl, hare, mallard, partridge, pheasant, rabbit, turkey, venison, wood pigeon, clams, cod, crab, dab, dover sole, grey mullet, gurnard, haddock, halibut, hake, herring, lemon sole, lobster, mackerel, monkfish, mussels, oysters, pilchard, plaice, pollack, prawns, red mullet, wild sea bass, sea bream, skate, squid, turbot and winkles.

NATURAL · FERMENTED · LIVING FOOD

RED CABBAGE AND BLACKBERRIES
WITH FERMENTED BEETS

Fermented beetroot:
2 tsp salt
300ml water
200g beetroot

2 tbsp apple cider vinegar
2 tbsp water
1 red cabbage, sliced
1 tsp salt
Handful of blackberries

To ferment the beetroot, first prepare the brine by dissolving the salt in the water. Peel and cut the beets into quarters, pack into a 500ml Kilner jar and cover with brine, leaving about 2.5cm of headspace. Press the beets down with a weight to keep them submerged.

Seal the jar with a tight lid and ferment for 2 to 3 weeks at room temperature. Once fermented, keep in the fridge.

Bring the apple cider vinegar and water to the boil in a large saucepan with a lid. Add the red cabbage and salt then cook on a low heat for 20 minutes until soft and tender. Mix the cooked cabbage with a small amount of beetroot brine to taste, then plate with the blackberries and a few pieces of the fermented beetroot.

ROASTED JERUSALEM ARTICHOKE WITH KALE AND ACV DRESSING

8 Jerusalem artichokes
1 tsp extra virgin olive oil
1 tsp salt
200g kale
1 tbsp Apple Cider Vinegar Living Dressing (see page 175)

Preheat the oven to 180°c. Wash, then lightly oil and salt the artichokes.
Place on a tray and cook in the oven for 20 minutes until soft. Meanwhile,
rinse the kale, remove the stalks and thinly slice the leaves.

Allow the cooked artichokes to cool before cutting into bite-size pieces. Massage
the dressing into the kale, then add the artichokes and serve warm.

CHARRED CHICORY WITH HAZELNUTS AND LEMON

2 heads of chicory
1 tbsp extra virgin olive oil
100g peeled and
activated hazelnuts
1 tbsp lemon juice
1 tsp salt
Freshly ground black
pepper, to taste

Preheat the oven to 180°c. Cut the chicory in half and place cut side down in an
ovenproof pan on a medium heat. Add the oil and lightly colour the chicory. Stir in
the hazelnuts then transfer the pan to the preheated oven for 10 minutes. Arrange in
a bowl, squeeze over the lemon juice then season with salt and pepper to finish.

       NATURAL • FERMENTED • LIVING FOOD

ROASTED BABY CARROTS
WITH SMOKED ALMOND AND KALE CRUMB

500g baby carrots
200g smoked almonds
200g kale
3 tbsp nutritional yeast

2 tbsp extra virgin olive oil
2 tbsp parsley
2 cloves of garlic
Salt and pepper, to taste

Preheat the oven to 160°c. Add everything except the carrots to a blender and pulse until a sandy consistency is achieved.

On a large baking tray, spread the mixture out evenly and bake in the preheated oven for 20 minutes until crispy. Leave to cool and turn the oven up to 180°c.

Roast the carrots on a baking tray lined with greasproof paper with a little olive oil for about 25 minutes until tender. Serve the carrots hot or cold in a bowl topped with the crispy almond and kale crumb.

PIQUILLO PEPPERS
WITH GOAT'S CURD AND KEFIR

200g piquillo peppers
100g goat's curd
50g kefir
½ tsp salt
Freshly ground black pepper, to taste

Drain the oil from the peppers and pat them dry. Mix the goat's curd and kefir together, season with salt and pepper then stuff each piquillo pepper with the mixture. Enjoy cold from the fridge. These can be made up to 3 days in advance.

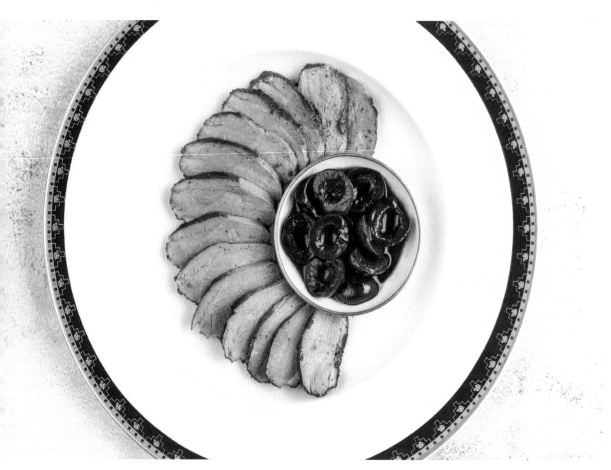

  NATURAL · FERMENTED · LIVING FOOD

ROASTED DUCK BREAST
WITH FERMENTED CHERRIES

Fermented cherries:
1 tsp salt
450ml filtered water
200g cherries

2 duck breasts
1 tbsp five spice (this is usually a mixture of ground fennel,
star anise, cinnamon, Szechuan peppercorns and clove)
1.5 tsp salt

To ferment the cherries, first prepare the brine by dissolving the salt in the water. Halve and destone the cherries, then pack them into a 500ml Kilner jar and cover with the brine, leaving about 2.5cm of headspace. Press the cherries down with a weight to keep them submerged if needed. Seal the jar with a tight lid and ferment for 5 to 7 days at room temperature. Once fermented, keep in the fridge.

Preheat the oven to 180°c. Score the skin of the duck breasts then rub in the five spice and salt. Place the duck skin side down in a cold pan on a medium heat. Press the duck gently into the pan to help crisp the skin and render the fat. Once the skin is crisp, place the duck on a rack in the preheated oven for about 12 minutes. Place a tray under the rack to catch the juices.

Once cooked, take the duck out of the oven and rest it for 10 minutes. Meanwhile, bring the fermented cherries and their brine to a gentle simmer in a wide saucepan. Place the rested duck breasts skin side up on the simmering cherries to get some heat and extra flavour into the duck. Slice the duck thinly and arrange on a plate with the cherries. Enjoy hot.

≋ ⚡ 🪷 💗 ❀ NATURAL · FERMENTED · LIVING FOOD

STEAMED LEEKS
WITH FERMENTED LEEKS AND ALMOND

2 large leeks
1 tbsp extra virgin olive oil
50g peeled, activated
and roasted almonds
Salt and pepper, to taste

Fermented leeks:
1 tbsp salt
300ml water
300g (about 2 large) leeks

To ferment the leeks, first prepare the brine by dissolving the salt in the water. Cut the leeks into 2cm slices and pack them into a 1L Kilner jar. Cover with the brine, leaving about 2.5cm of headspace. Weigh the leeks to keep them submerged if needed. Seal the jar with a tight lid and ferment for 10 to 14 days at room temperature. After the fermentation period, store in the fridge.

Cook the whole leeks in a steamer for 4 minutes. Remove and cut into 2cm slices. In a frying pan on high heat, colour the leeks in the olive oil. Pulse the almonds in a blender, until they have a crumb-like consistency. In a mixing bowl, combine the fermented and cooked leeks and dress in a little of the leek brine, olive oil and almond crumb. Serve warm in a bowl.

WILD RED RICE WITH PARSLEY
AND FERMENTED LEMON ZEST

200g wild red rice
1 tbsp extra virgin olive oil
400ml water
2 tbsp fresh parsley, chopped
1 tbsp lemon juice
1 tsp salt

Fermented lemon:
100g unwaxed lemon zest
½ tsp salt

To ferment the lemon zest, combine it with the salt and pack into a 250ml Kilner jar. Leave at room temperature for 10-14 days before using. Rinse the rice under running water, then drain thoroughly. In a large saucepan, heat the oil then add the rice. Stir for 2 minutes, then add the water and bring to the boil. Lower the heat and cover the pan. Cook the rice for 35 minutes, then remove from the heat and leave to rest for 10 minutes. Stir the parsley, lemon juice, salt and some fermented lemon zest to taste into the rice. Eat hot or cold.

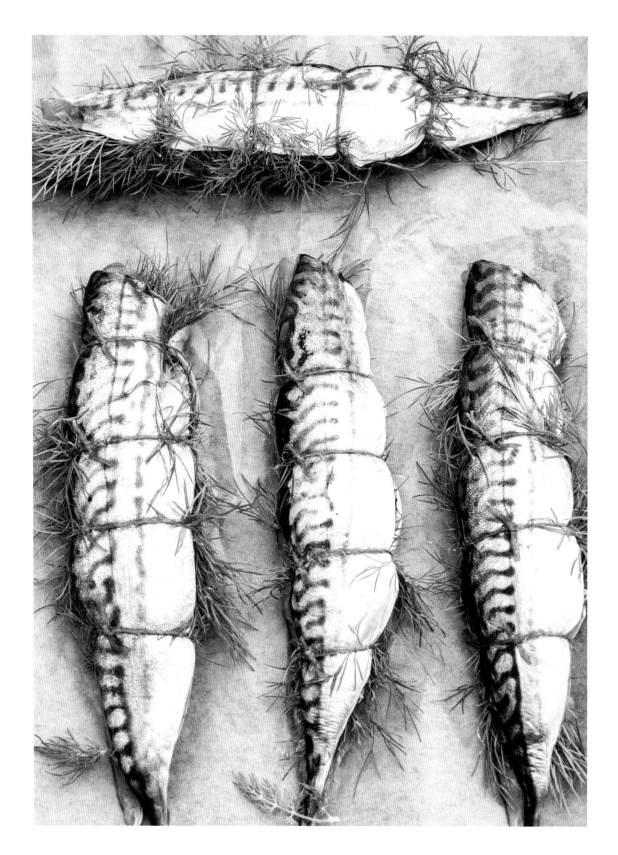

STUFFED MACKEREL
WITH APPLE AND DILL

2 whole mackerel
1 tsp salt
1 bunch of dill
2 tbsp extra virgin olive oil
4 Granny Smith apples
Freshly ground black pepper, to taste

Preheat the oven to 180°c.

Season the flesh of the mackerel with the salt and stuff with
the dill. Use butchers' twine to secure the fish.

Oil the outside of the fish and wrap in greaseproof paper. Place
in the preheated oven to cook for 8 to 10 minutes.

Cut the apples into matchsticks. Serve the mackerel topped with apple, drizzled
with a generous amount of extra virgin olive oil and seasoned with black pepper.

High Tip

Ask your fishmonger to butterfly and pin bone the mackerel for you.

ROASTED HOKKAIDO SQUASH WITH ZA'ATAR

2 Hokkaido squash (butternut squash is a good alternative)
1 tbsp extra virgin olive oil
1 tsp salt
1 tbsp za'atar

Preheat the oven to 180°c. Peel the squash and cut into 2cm slices. On a flat baking tray, oil and salt the squash, lay flat and bake for 35 minutes.

Plate by sprinkling the za'atar over the roasted squash. Eat hot.

BUCKWHEAT COUSCOUS WITH APPLE CIDER VINEGAR AND PARSLEY DRESSING

200g buckwheat
400ml water
2 tbsp Apple Cider Vinegar Living Dressing (see page 175)
2 tbsp fresh parsley, chopped
1 tbsp fresh chives, chopped
1 tbsp fresh mint, chopped
1 tsp salt
Freshly ground black pepper, to taste

Rinse and drain the buckwheat. In a medium saucepan, toast the buckwheat on a low heat to give an even brown colour. Cover with the water and bring to the boil, then reduce the heat and simmer for 10 to 12 minutes. Drain off any excess liquid and allow to cool. In a bowl, mix the buckwheat with the dressing, herbs, salt and pepper. Serve cold.

NATURAL · FERMENTED · LIVING FOOD

MISO GLAZED KING OYSTER MUSHROOMS WITH SHAVED FENNEL SALAD

4 large king oyster mushrooms
1 bulb of fennel
1 tbsp miso
1 tsp fennel seeds
Salt and pepper, to taste

Preheat the oven to 180°c.

Cut the mushrooms in half lengthways. Slice the fennel thinly on a mandoline.
In a bowl, mix the miso with the fennel seeds.

In a hot griddle pan, cook the mushrooms flat side down. Using a pastry brush, glaze the
mushrooms with the miso and fennel seeds then bake in the preheated oven for 5 minutes.

To serve, lay out the mushrooms on a plate, garnish with the shaved
fennel and drizzle over any leftover miso glaze. Season to taste.

WINTER

Plants: Jerusalem artichoke, brussels sprouts, romanesco, January king cabbage, cavolo nero, celeriac, kale, leeks, forced rhubarb and truffles.

Protein: game birds and wild fowl, venison, hare, clams, cockles, dab, dover sole, gurnard, haddock, halibut, hake, langoustine, lemon sole, lobster, mackerel, mussels, oysters, red mullet, scallops, sea bream, skate, turbot and winkles.

    NATURAL · FERMENTED · LIVING FOOD

SPROUTED SPELT PORRIDGE WITH WILD MUSHROOM AND CHIVE

200ml water
2 tbsp dried trompette mushrooms
½ onion, finely chopped
1 clove of garlic, minced
2 tbsp butter

200g sprouted spelt
500ml mushroom stock
1 tsp extra virgin olive oil
50g wild mushrooms
1 tbsp fresh chives, chopped

In a medium-size saucepan, boil the water and add the dried trompette mushrooms. Take off the heat and leave them to rehydrate for 15 to 20 minutes. Rinse well.

Meanwhile, sweat the onion and garlic in 1 tablespoon of the butter then add the trompettes. Add the spelt and pour in the mushroom stock. Cook for 25 minutes, stirring every so often as the spelt is likely to stick to the pan. Finish with the remaining butter.

Heat the oil in a frying pan and cook the wild mushrooms with a pinch of salt for 2 minutes. Transfer the spelt porridge to a bowl and garnish with wild mushrooms and chopped chives.

CHARRED AND STEAMED SPROUTING ONIONS

8 large sprouted onions
2 tbsp kombucha vinegar
1 tsp salt

Clean the root end of your onions and peel the outer layer away.
Using a bamboo steamer, cook half of the onions for 20 minutes.

Heat a frying pan and slowly char the rest of the onions until the outside is deep brown and caramelised but the inside is soft and sweet.

Season the steamed onions with the kombucha vinegar and salt then combine them with the charred onions. Serve hot.

COFFEE KOMBUCHA
GLAZED PARSNIPS

500g baby parsnips
200g Coffee Kombucha (see page 43)
1 tsp extra virgin olive oil
½ tsp salt

Wash and cut each parsnip in half lengthways. Heat a shallow frying pan with
a little oil and salt, then colour the parsnips in the pan cut side down.

When the parsnips are golden brown, add the coffee kombucha.
Simmer the kombucha until it reduces and coats the parsnips. Serve hot.

SHIRATAKI NOODLES
WITH MISO AND WINTER RADISH

200g shirataki noodles
1 tbsp light miso
1 tbsp tamari
1 tbsp sesame oil

1 winter radish, sliced
1 tsp fresh coriander, chopped
1 tsp fresh chives, chopped
Salt and pepper, to taste

Thoroughly rinse the noodles until the water is odourless and runs clear.

In a large bowl, mix the miso, tamari and sesame oil together, then
let the noodles sit in the sauce to soak up the flavours.

Plate the soaked noodles and scatter with the radish, herbs and seasoning to serve.

  NATURAL • FERMENTED • LIVING FOOD

GRILLED PRAWNS
WITH PARSLEY AND THYME

½ onion
1 clove of garlic
Fresh chillies, to taste
2 tbsp butter
1 tbsp extra virgin olive oil
1 tsp fresh thyme, chopped
8 large prawns
½ tsp salt
2 tbsp fresh parsley, chopped
1 tbsp lemon juice

In a medium-size pan sweat the onion, garlic and however much
chopped fresh chilli you like in the butter over a medium heat.

Preheat a griddle pan or heavy frying pan. Oil the griddle then add the thyme
so it releases the flavour into the oil. Once the pan is smoking hot, add the
prawns and cook on a high heat for about 2 minutes on each side.

Remove the pan from the heat and rest the prawns in the hot pan for
a further 4 minutes so they gently finish cooking through.

Coat the prawns with the chilli and garlic mixture, season with salt, garnish
with chopped parsley and serve with a squeeze of lemon juice.

TEMPEH BOURGUIGNON

500g tempeh, diced
50g onion
2 cloves of garlic
1 tbsp extra virgin olive oil
200ml red wine
1 tbsp fresh thyme, chopped
1 tsp salt
Freshly ground black pepper, to taste

Preheat the oven to 150°c. Heat an ovenproof pot or dish, then colour the tempeh, onion and garlic in the oil. Be careful not to burn the garlic, keeping it moving around the pot.

Deglaze with the wine and then let it reduce. Add the thyme then transfer the pot to the preheated oven to and cook uncovered for 1 hour.

Season the bourguignon with salt and pepper to taste then serve hot.

BRAISED BEEF AND ONIONS
WITH WINTER SAVORY

500g onions, sliced

3 tbsp apple cider vinegar

1kg feather blade beef

1 tbsp salt

500ml beef stock

2 tbsp fresh winter savory, chopped

1 tbsp fresh parsley, chopped

1 tbsp fresh chives, chopped

1 tbsp yoghurt

Preheat the oven to 100°c. In a ovenproof pan big enough to fit all the beef, caramelise the sliced onions in oil slowly, stirring frequently until they are evenly golden brown. Deglaze the pan with the apple cider vinegar.

Heat a separate pan and colour the outside of the feather blade with salt and a little oil. Transfer the meat to the pan of onions and deglaze the other pan with the beef stock.

Pour the hot beef stock into the pan of onions and beef, add the savory and cover the pot with a lid. Cook in the preheated oven for 12 to 14 hours until the meat falls apart.

Strain the liquid through a colander into a clean saucepan pan and reduce it to a sticky glaze.

Allow the beef to cool in the pan but keep the lid on to hold as much moisture in as possible. Once the beef is cool enough to handle, pick it down into small pieces and stir it into the glaze.

Reheat the beef in the glaze and then plate with plenty of herbs scattered on top and a spoonful of yoghurt or creme fraiche.

BRAISED BLACK RICE
WITH FENNEL AND CHIVE

200g black short grain rice
1 tbsp fennel seeds
500ml water
1 tsp salt

50g Classic Kraut (see page 53)
Salt and black pepper, to taste
1 tbsp fresh chives, chopped

Soak the black rice for 30 minutes then rinse well and drain. Meanwhile, toast the fennel seeds in a hot dry pan for 2 minutes. Bring the water to the boil with the salt and fennel seeds.

Place the drained rice into the boiling water, keeping the pan uncovered. Bring the water back to the boil, then put a lid on the pan, turn the heat down very low heat and cook for 25 minutes. Take the rice off the heat after this time and leave covered for a further 10 minutes.

Should there be any excess liquid, strain the rice and allow to cool before stirring the kraut into it. Season with salt and pepper, garnish with the chopped chives and serve.

CELERIAC AND APPLE SLAW

1 celeriac
1 Granny Smith apple
1 tbsp Apple Cider Vinegar

Living Dressing (see page 175)
1 tbsp fresh chives, chopped
½ tsp salt

Peel and grate or julienne the celeriac and apple. Place them into a mixing bowl with the dressing, chives and salt. Stir to combine and taste to check the seasoning. Enjoy cold and keep in the fridge for up to 3 days.

NATURAL · FERMENTED · LIVING FOOD

ROASTED PUMPKIN, CAVOLO NERO AND HAZELNUTS

1 pumpkin
1 tsp extra virgin olive oil
1 tsp salt
1 bunch of cavolo nero (also known as Italian or Tuscan kale)
50g activated hazelnuts

Preheat the oven to 180°c. Peel and deseed the pumpkin, then cut the flesh into 4cm cubes and roll them in the oil and salt. On a flat baking tray, roast the pumpkin in the oven for around 30 minutes.

Cut the cavolo nero lengthways on either side of the stalk to remove it and end up with two long pieces. Turn the oven temperature down to 150°c.

Lightly oil the cavolo nero and hazelnuts, place them into the cooler oven on a baking tray and bake for 10 minutes. Top the roasted pumpkin with the cavolo nero and hazelnuts, plate and enjoy hot.

SALSIFY, WATERCRESS AND LEMON

8 sticks of salsify
2 tbsp lemon juice
2 tbsp water
1 tbsp butter

1 tsp salt
1 bunch of watercress
1 tbsp fresh parsley, chopped

Peel your salsify. It is best to use gloves for this. Once peeled, it will turn brown very quickly so combine the lemon juice and water to drop the salsify into as you go. Melt the butter in a frying pan on a medium heat until it's bubbling and starting to brown slightly.

Add the salsify to the pan, season with salt and keep it moving around the pan to create an even colour. Once tender and golden brown, slice at an angle, mix with the watercress and parsley and serve.

   NATURAL · FERMENTED · LIVING FOOD

PAN SEARED SCALLOPS IN LEMON BUTTER

4 hand-dived scallops, in the shell with roe
1 tbsp butter
1 lemon
1 tbsp fresh parsley, chopped
Salt and pepper, to taste

Using a knife, remove the scallops from their shells. Remove the skirt then wash the scallops and roe in ice cold water.

Dry the roe in a low oven or a dehydrator at 56°c for 24 hours. When completely dry, blend the roe to a powder in a food processor and set aside.

Preheat a frying pan. Cook the scallops on the first side for for 1 minute, then pull the pan off the heat, flip the scallops over and add the butter. Baste the scallops in the melted butter to finish cooking.

To serve, place scallops back in their shells then season with the roe powder, squeeze over some lemon juice and scatter with chopped parsley or a few micro herbs. Add salt and pepper to taste.

KIDS AND THE 5 K
Budding Taste Buds

We support young children by introducing a wide variety of vegetables and fruits to your child's diet as soon as they start eating solids. If your child is older, not to worry: you can always introduce new foods at any age. Just remember if at first you don't succeed, keep trying! Introducing new foods takes time and patience but with a bit of commitment your children will end up with well-rounded palates and curiosity about trying new foods.

HOW DO WE INTRODUCE OUR CHILDREN TO FERMENTED FOOD?

Younger children often prefer sweeter tasting foods, especially when given a choice. It is difficult to get a child to eat broccoli after a bowl of sugary cereal or to have soup after a packet of biscuits. We always suggest offering more nutritious options first, especially when they are hungry!

It is important for kids to see everyone in the family eating the same food. The family meal concept encourages children to try different dishes as they see others at the table enjoying themselves. In our experience, a slightly simplified approach is all that is needed to introduce children to fermented foods.

WHILE EVERY CHILD IS DIFFERENT, HERE ARE SOME OF OUR TIPS:

SIMPLER FOOD

We think that children can and should eat the same food as adults. When starting out, kids often prefer to see the components separated: some veg, some protein and a side dish. Once familiar with the meal they may be more open to a mixed plate. Try non-spicy marinades to add flavour and offer sauces on the side; kids love to dip!

DO NOT HIDE THE SWEETNESS

Food that is marketed for children is often full of sugar and contains highly processed fats or flavourings. Yoghurts, cereals, and children's biscuits often do not contain many nutrients. We would recommend serving dishes such as yoghurts, bakes or puddings in their most natural form without sugar. Let your child sprinkle on some cinnamon, add a dash of vanilla or drizzle over some honey or high-grade maple syrup. It is good learning for your child to figure out which ingredient changes the taste and how much sweetness they want. If your young child does not eat at a meal don't stress about it; there is usually no problem with letting your child get a little hungry. Don't rush to make a sandwich as they will be more likely to work up a healthy appetite and eat a wholesome meal next time! Food is at the core of our nurturing instincts. Sometimes playing a game or going for a cuddle is more satisfying than a meal.

SNACKING

Prepare some healthy snacks to keep in the refrigerator or to have on the go. We like hummus with carrot and cucumber sticks. Try sprinkling a bit of dark chocolate or hemp and chia seeds on top of a berry kefir smoothie. Apple slices with nut butter or a few raisins, if you don't mind the sugar, are also good options. Be thoughtful with snack times, as too soon before a meal will diminish your child's interest in eating at the regular time. If they ask for a snack right before the meal, offer some veggies!

SMOOTHIES

Smoothies are an easy way to give your child a mixture of great nutrients. Let your child help you load up the blender with greens (spinach or kale blend well), a handful of berries, chia seeds, some kefir, and blitz!

FERMENTS

We find that children will actually eat and enjoy the 5 K! Kefir can be mixed with berries, and most children love a sip of kombucha or kefir water. Although the alcohol content is meant to be minimal, we do not recommend allowing your child to drink a whole bottle.

DON'T BE TOO STRICT WITH YOUR CHILDREN

The most important lesson for your children is to have a relaxed, wholesome approach to eating. Make it fun, let them help you make the food and let them serve and feed themselves. Children learn through play, feeling the textures of the different ingredients and mashing things up while cooking. We wouldn't recommend turning food into play items as children should respect the origin and value of food, but they need to experience food as colour, texture and taste.

The more involved they are in the process of preparing and serving a meal the more interested they will be in eating and enjoying it!

EAT WITH YOUR CHILDREN

Many children do not have the experience of a regular family meal. They eat in front of the TV, while playing on their tablets or on their way to school. Make time for a family meal and talk with, or even better, listen to your children. It is best practice for children to be mindful of mealtimes and not get the time for eating muddled with play or TV time. Eating at the table allows children to be aware of what and how much they are eating with less chance of mindless overeating. We recommend avoiding the use of food and treats as a reward, because this can lead to potential emotional eating challenges in future. As always, we tread lightly and would not argue against the occasional treat of pizza in front of the telly at a special occasion, just don't let it become a habit.

TALK ABOUT THE FOOD

It can be a fun, educational and mindful practice to make the ingredient and its journey to your plate a topic of conversation. Where does this vegetable grow? When does it get planted? In which season does it get harvested? Is it a root? How high does it grow? Where does this animal live? What does it eat? What else could we make with this? Should we try this dish next time? Will you help me make it?

MINDFULNESS

Take a moment to think about and appreciate all the time and effort that has gone into growing and preparing the food that we eat and how what we eat impacts our bodies. Good food can nourish, help to grow and heal our children. For mindfulness and a feeling of being present, it can be a wonderful practice to take a moment before the family meal just to appreciate the food and being together.

TEENAGERS

Older kids often enjoy making the ferments. Massaging the kraut until it yields a juice, shredding the vegetables, and feeding the sourdough can be really fun. As with adults, the teenagers get a different joy from eating food that they helped to grow and make. Sprouting seeds is fun for all ages and many kids who do not like salad at first will enjoy eating the sprouts once they have watched them grow from seeds.

KIDS' RECIPE IDEAS

Fermented carrots and cucumbers are great for kids and combine well with a green kefir dip made with spinach, chives or dill.

Many children will eat Classic Kraut (see page 53) on its own or with a sausage. Once they are used to the taste, they might even enjoy a glass of the brine every now and then, especially when the weather is hot. Half a sour cucumber is also a favourite snack on hot summer days.

Dairy Kefir (see page 28) mixed or blended with berries is lovely and an easy winner with most kids! Or you could try a winter version with apple compote, consisting of simmered cubed apple and a cinnamon stick. Depending on the apple variety it should be sweet enough on its own, but you can always add a drizzle of honey or a few drops of stevia.

A great way to use up leftover grains is to make a savoury pancake. Mix 2 eggs and 1 or 2 handfuls of cooked grains like quinoa with some chopped up spinach and cheese, then pan fry spoonfuls of the batter until golden.

A combination of zoodles and Kamut spaghetti is a fun way of turning your kids' favourite dish into a nutritious meal. Or you could try and add a blended broccoli and kale green sauce to chickpea pasta!

The High Cultured Toastie (see page 111) is a staple favourite for adults and children alike and a great way to offer different ferments like kraut or kimchi in one quick and tasty dish.

Mini crust-less quiche is an easy packable meal or snack. Fill a greased or non-stick muffin tin with a mixture of cooked and chopped vegetables; this is a great job for little hands. Sprinkle some feta or olives on top then pour a mixture of beaten eggs and creme fraiche into each one and bake in the oven until they are set.

Finger sandwiches are always a win with kids. Try thinly sliced toasted sourdough with a spread of cream kefir and cured or hot smoked salmon with cucumber rounds on the side.

Berry jelly is a great dessert for kids. All you need is a handful of frozen berries, some gelatine and sometimes a bit of stevia blended together to make a lovely gut-healthy jelly. Try our Low Carb Brownie too (see page 189) and indulge with your children. Remember, dark chocolate is a superfood and coconut oil contains a bomb of nutrients!

ENTERTAINING
AT HOME

Snacks and party food are a fun opportunity to play with flavour combinations and the varying textures of food. Depending on the mood of the occasion, we like to use different forms of presentation. Sharing platters create an inclusive family feel and espresso cups or little spoons can be fun for tasting comfort foods in appetising tiny portions. Quail eggs on kale with biotic mayo and a tad of curried kraut is a fun combination, and our devilled eggs are a supercharged and pretty-to-look-at treat!

ENTERTAINING AT HOME

Tiny bowl food could be served in espresso cups: think comfort food with a twist, like cocktail sausage and white kraut or mini mashed potato with activated tamari seeds and parmesan shavings. Soups are a great appetiser and look pretty in a small cup. Try broccoli with chilli oil, dahl with dukkha or mushroom soup with dehydrated kimchi.

It is also easy to use vegetables as base for snacks. Try chicory or cucumber with creamy kefir and a sliver of salmon with dill, or carrot sticks with a trio of hummus. Cavolo nero or kale chips with sea salt and a sprinkle of turmeric are a great crunchy snack on their own or decoration for any dish.

FERMENTED MOCKTAILS

We love probiotic mocktails. Make your own ginger or turmeric 'bug' and add a spoonful to your choice of kombucha, kefir or just water. It will create beautifully flavoured and refreshing summer sodas. Throw in some fresh fruit and mint to make wonderful mocktails.

You can add alcohol in different measures; kombucha mixes well with sparkling wine. Try a spoonful of pomegranate seeds or a few strawberries and slices of cucumber with fresh mint for a summer Pimm's-style drink!

Some pureed fruit such as seasonal peaches make an indulgent kombucha champagne not unlike a bellini. You could add some alcohol-free spirit (such as Three Spirits or Seedlip) or opt for the real cocktail taste and add a shot of locally made gin or vodka. For a taste of the British summertime, serve orange marmalade gin with a slice of apple and pear over plenty of ice or Welsh gin infused with hand-picked seaweed from the Celtic. There is some research that shows the effects of alcohol can be mitigated by the live bacteria contained in kombucha, but we would gently remind you to tread lightly: go big on the booch and light on the booze!

If you fancy making your own kombucha vinegar, the next step could be to make your own shrubs, also referred to as drinking vinegar. You can buy shrubs made with a variety of different vinegars for different flavours, but making your own is very simple. They also make great gifts! Apple cider vinegar is an easy ready-made base for a shrub that has a pleasant and mild taste.

HOW TO MAKE SHRUBS (DRINKING VINEGAR)

Shrubs are made from equal parts vinegar and sugar (we recommend coconut sugar) mixed with fruit and flavourings such as ginger or vanilla. The mixture steeps in the fridge for a couple of days until the liquid takes on the fruit flavour. It tastes great with kombucha or sparkling water and makes an extra gut-healthy drink.

HOT METHOD

Begin by making a simple syrup of water and coconut sugar by combining equal parts water and sugar. Stir constantly until the sugar has dissolved, then add fruit and any herbs or spices. Simmer to release the juices and flavours into the syrup. Add the vinegar after cooling and just before bottling (it preserves the live bacteria in the vinegar). Bottle and allow to set in the fridge for a few days. More coconut sugar or vinegar can be added to taste.

COLD METHOD

Use equal amounts of fruit and vinegar in a jar with a tight fitting lid and shake vigorously for about 30 seconds. Allow the mixture to infuse at room temperature for about a week and give it a good shake once a day. Strain out the solids then add half the weight of the fruit in coconut sugar and shake until it has completely dissolved. Refrigerate for about a week and add more coconut sugar or vinegar to taste.

  NATURAL · FERMENTED · LIVING FOOD

DEVILLED EGGS

6 free-range eggs at room temperature (quail eggs could be used instead)
3 tbsp Biotic Mayo (see page 178)
2 tsp Dijon mustard
1 tsp sea salt flakes
¼ tsp smoked paprika, plus extra for decorating
A few drops of Living Hot Sauce (optional, see page 176)
2 tbsp extra virgin olive oil
2-3 tbsp filtered water
1 tsp Activated Dukkah (see page 184)
2 tsp fresh chives, finely chopped

Bring some water to the boil in a large saucepan. Once boiling, add the eggs one by one to the pan and bring back to the boil. Boil for 1 minute, then turn the heat off and leave the eggs to stand in the pan for 12 minutes. While you're waiting for the eggs to cook, fill a large bowl with very cold water, and throw in a handful of ice cubes if you have them.

As soon as the eggs have had their 12 minutes, transfer them into the cold water and leave for 15 minutes – no longer – before peeling patiently and carefully. Halve the eggs lengthways, then gently prise the yolk out of each half and pop them into a mixing bowl. Place the halved whites on a plate.

Add the mayo, Dijon mustard, salt and paprika to the egg yolks, then shake a few drops of hot sauce on top if you like. Stir and mash everything together with a fork, then blend with a stick blender or in a food processor. Add the oil and blend again until smooth. The mixture will be very thick. Taste to check the seasoning and see whether you want this any hotter. By hand, stir in as much of the filtered water as you need to get a piping consistency.

Spoon the golden mixture into a piping bag with a star-shaped nozzle, making sure it is densely packed at the bottom of the bag. Then pipe away, filling the hollowed-out whites with golden rosettes. You can fill the whites using a pair of teaspoons instead. Sprinkle with the extra paprika, dukkah and chopped chives to serve.

BEETROOT ON GOOD GUT CROUTONS

50g goat's cheese
1 tbsp miso paste
1 tbsp light soy sauce
10 thin slices of Good Gut Bread, toasted
or dehydrated (see page 107)
2 cooked beetroot, finely diced

In a bowl, whip the goat's cheese, miso paste and light soy sauce until
completely combined and smooth. Spread the whipped goat's cheese on
the slices of Good Gut Bread and top it with finely diced beetroot.

FERMENTED MUSHROOM
SAN CHOY BOW

400g chestnut mushrooms
20ml tamari
40g peanut or sesame oil
1 lime, juiced
1 tsp maple syrup
2 pak choi
15g activated peanuts (see page 18)
Fresh coriander and spring onions, to garnish

Marinate the mushrooms in a 2% brine for 5 days. When they are ready, whisk
the tamari, oil, lime juice and maple syrup together to make the dressing.
Separate the leaves of the pak choi then top each one with mushrooms
and peanuts. Garnish with coriander and spring onions to taste.

CRACKERS FOR CURRY KRAUT AND KEFIR SOUR CREAM

40g buckwheat flour
60g sunflower seeds
60g pumpkin seeds
30g chia seeds
30g sesame seeds
30g ground flax seeds
60g mixed whole brown
and golden flax seeds

2 tbsp extra virgin olive oil
80ml hot water
Dried herbs such as oregano,
rosemary, thyme or a mix
like Herbes de Provence
Salt and pepper, to taste

Preheat the oven to 160°c. Combine all the dry ingredients in a large bowl, then pour in the oil and hot water. Add herbs and seasoning to taste. Stir to combine everything then leave the mixture to rest for 15 minutes. Roll out thinly between sheets of greaseproof paper, transfer onto trays and bake in the preheated oven for 20 to 25 minutes until golden brown. Allow to cool and break into bite-size pieces.

Spread some Kefir Sour Cream (see below) onto the crackers, add Curried Kraut (see page 53) and garnish with fresh herbs of your choice.

KEFIR SOUR CREAM

200ml organic heavy cream
15g kefir grains

Pour the cream into a mason jar with the kefir grains. Seal the jar and leave out of direct sunlight for 24 hours, then let it sit in your fridge for another day or two. Remove the grains before using.

  NATURAL • FERMENTED • LIVING FOOD

CAJUN CHICKEN SKEWERS

4 boneless chicken thighs
4 large spring onions, cut into batons
2 tbsp thyme, chopped
2 tbsp garlic, chopped
2 tbsp maple syrup
1 tsp smoked chilli flakes
1 tsp smoked paprika
2 tbsp coconut oil, melted
Pinch of salt

Cut the chicken into 4cm cubes. Blend the remaining ingredients into a smooth paste.

Coat the chicken in the paste, cover and marinate in the fridge overnight.

Thread the marinated chicken pieces onto soaked skewers and cook in a hot frying pan until crispy on the edges and cooked through.

Serve with your choice of mild or spicy dipping sauce.

   NATURAL · FERMENTED · LIVING FOOD

BABA GANOUSH WITH
CAVOLO NERO CRISPS

100g cavolo nero
2 aubergines
30ml extra virgin olive oil
2 lemons, zested and juiced
Pinch of cayenne pepper
Pinch of salt

Preheat the oven to 160°c. Remove the thick stems of the cavolo nero,
then lightly oil and season the leaves. Lay them on a tray and bake in the
preheated oven for 15 minutes until crispy and golden brown.

Poke some holes into the skin of the aubergines with a fork then place directly on the flame
of the hob until fully blackened and soft. You can also do this under an extremely hot grill.

Halve the blackened aubergines, scrape out the flesh and blend until smooth.
Slowly add the olive oil to the blender, then the lemon zest, juice, cayenne and
salt. Taste and adjust the seasoning as needed, then transfer to a bowl.

Serve the baba ganoush with the kale crisps for dipping.

CAULIFLOWER BITES

1 medium cauliflower
50g unsweetened shredded coconut
50g sourdough breadcrumbs

Batter:
120ml plant milk of your choice
70g almond flour
2 cloves of garlic, minced
1 lime, zested and juiced
1½ tsp ground turmeric
1 tsp smoked sweet paprika
1 tsp ground cumin
½ tsp salt
Living Hot Sauce, for dipping (see page 176)

Preheat the oven to 200°c. Remove the leaves and the stalk
of the cauliflower and cut into bite-size florets.

In a bowl, whisk together the plant milk, almond flour, garlic, lime zest and juice,
turmeric, paprika, cumin and salt to create a thick batter. If the batter is too runny,
add a little more almond flour. Add the cauliflower florets and coat well.

Mix the shredded coconut and sourdough crumbs together in a separate bowl.
Coat each battered cauliflower bite generously in the sourdough and coconut
crumb. Set aside on a baking tray lined with greaseproof paper.

Leave plenty of space between the cauliflower bites so they crisp up while baking.
Bake the cauliflower bites for 25-30 minutes, flipping halfway through
so they cook evenly until crisp and golden. Serve immediately
with Living Hot Sauce for dipping (see page 176).

    NATURAL · FERMENTED · LIVING FOOD

TEMPEH SPOONS OR SKEWERS

You can get creative here and combine different recipes in bite-size portions:
these marinated tempeh cubes with half a quail egg and a dab of miso
will make a tasty appetiser that you and your gut bacteria will enjoy!
This recipe uses skewers for another great party food alternative.

½ tsp chilli powder
1 tsp sweet smoked paprika
1 tsp ground cinnamon
2 tsp ground cumin
2 cloves of garlic, minced
1 lemon, juiced
100g yoghurt
400g tempeh
2 tbsp Activated Dukkah (see page 184)
Pinch of sea salt and black pepper to taste

Preheat the oven to 200°c. Add all the spices, garlic and lemon juice to the
yoghurt and mix well. Cut the tempeh into bite-size cubes and coat in the yoghurt
marinade. Leave for at least 1 hour, but the longer it marinates the more flavour
it absorbs. In the meantime, soak a handful of wooden skewers in water.

Thread 2 or 3 marinated tempeh cubes onto each soaked wooden
skewer and cook under the grill in the oven for 25 to 30 minutes,
turning halfway so each side cooks evenly, until golden and crisp.

Sprinkle the tempeh with the activated dukkah and serve warm.

HERB CRUSTED CASHEW 'CHEESE' BALLS

Vegan 'cheese' made from nuts is a favourite for many vegans. Try blitzing two parts kraut with one part macadamia nuts, or kimchi and Brazil nuts with a little brine for a variety of fermented toppings on a slice of bread or crackers.

200g raw unsalted cashews
3 tbsp unwaxed lemon zest
3 tbsp lemon juice
2 tbsp coconut oil
1 clove of garlic
1 tsp white miso paste
½ tsp sea salt flakes
2 tsp finely chopped dill, chives or other herbs of your choice
Toasted and chopped nuts and seeds of your choice

Soak the cashews in cold water for up to 4 hours. Once soaked, rinse and drain the cashews thoroughly and put them into the food processor. Add the lemon zest and juice, coconut oil, minced garlic, miso paste, salt and black pepper to taste.

Blend the cashew mixture until creamy and very smooth, adding up to 2 tablespoons of water if necessary. Taste and adjust the seasoning as needed.

Empty the mixture into a cheesecloth, wrap tightly in a ball and place it in a strainer over a bowl. Leave to drain overnight.

Remove the cashew cheese from the cloth and shape it into little balls. Gently coat each ball in herbs or nuts and seeds for extra crunch. Refrigerate until ready to serve.

These are lovely served on a board with crackers (see page 301), Curried Kraut (see page 53) and your choice of seasonal vegetable crudités.

MINI DESSERT BITES

To complete your finger food buffet, you can easily adjust our desserts from the Snacks section (see page 186) by cutting cakes and brownies into smaller portions.

Put small pieces of our Low Carb Brownie (see page 189) into mini paper cases and garnish with chilli flakes.

Here are some additional ideas for mini desserts:

FLORENTINE BISCUITS

An easy pastry with nuts, dark chocolate and candied orange peel as the main ingredients. Cut them as large or small as needed.

LEMON POSSETS AND FLOATING ISLANDS

These can both be served in espresso cups. Garnish with or hide some of your fermented blueberries in the dessert for a special treat. Fresh mint leaves add a refreshing touch.

MINI FRUIT CRUMBLES

A complete eye-catcher at every party. Use a mixture of different nuts for the crumble toppings and garnish with a teaspoon of Kefir Ice Cream (see page 35) with a dash of cinnamon on top.

TAPIOCA PUDDING

Made from small tapioca pearls, prepared with coconut cream and garnished with any seasonal fresh fruit. An easy and satisfying dessert.

GLOSSARY

Being informed about the best food to eat is a great step towards making food your best medicine. This A to Z explanation of goodness will help you in your quest.

ALMOND MILK – Whether you are dairy-free or not, almond milk is yummy. It's made from a process of soaking and blending almonds. We recommend looking out for local almonds to avoid the carbon footprint. It's delicious in our hot Superfood specials or as a dairy milk substitute in coffees or lattes.

ARTISANAL – This means food grown, sourced and prepared in smaller quantities by people who are passionate, knowledgeable, and skilled in traditional recipes and methods.

BEE POLLEN - Bee pollen has almost every nutrient we'll ever need. It helps strengthen us against allergies, is rich in vitamins, minerals, proteins, lipids, fatty acids, enzymes, carotenoids and bioflavonoids. This equates to an antibacterial, antifungal and antiviral buzz that strengthens capillaries, reduces inflammation, boosts immunity and more. Add a bee pollen boost in your next smoothie to up the nutritional value.

BLACK PEPPER – Piperine, vitamins C and A, flavonoids, carotenes and other antioxidants give black pepper a good rap. Via the taste buds, it sends a signal to the stomach to produce digestive acid that breaks down proteins and is said to boost metabolism. It also makes turmeric bioavailable so your body can use it more effectively.

BONE BROTH - Drinking bone broth is a great way to use food as medicine. It's high in collagen, a structural protein found in skin and other connective tissues, and famous for healing and sealing the gut. When the gut is healthy it takes care of 90% of digestion and assimilation. It's touted as one of the best beauty foods to benefit skin, hair and nails. Our High bone broth is totally pure with no chemicals or nasties and uses the age-old value of time to extract the goodness.

BUCKWHEAT – This nutty, fluffy, foodstuff is gluten-free and neither a cereal grain nor related to the wheat family. It's actually a seed but often treated as a grain. Buckwheat's starch, protein, fat and mineral composition has caught the interest of food scientists as it offers almost all the essential amino acids in the best proportions, especially lysine. It also has good antioxidant and anti-inflammatory properties, loads of B-complex vitamins as well as copper and magnesium. Copper supports red blood cells while magnesium relaxes the blood vessels leading to the brain and is known to help alleviate depression and headaches.

CHLOROPHYLL – Chlorophyll is the green pigment in plants that facilitates photosynthesis. It's a gift from nature! It has been credited with keeping cravings in check and is so cleansing that it even gets rid of bad body odours. It seems to attract toxins, bind to them and eliminate them. People love chlorophyll as preventive cancer agent and powerful antioxidant. It nourishes our cells by transporting oxygen and cleansing toxins.

CINNAMON – Spicy, warming, balancing and satiating, there's so much to love about cinnamon. It balances blood sugar levels and is a goodie when it comes to brain health. If you are aiming to cut back on sugar or coffee, add a sprinkle of cinnamon to your food and drink. It might reduce your craving and take the edge off your jitters!

COCONUT OIL – Coconut oil is great for improving digestion, helping with weight loss, better brain function, skin health, building immunity and regulating blood sugar levels. This multi-tasking good fat is also good for baking and frying as it has a very high smoke point. You could try and use coconut oil for the ancient Indian tradition of 'oil pulling': swirling a spoonful of coconut oil in the mouth first thing in the morning.

COCONUT SUGAR – Also called nectar or blossom sugar, this caramel coloured sweetener comes from coconut blossom. It has a more favourable glycaemic index than cane sugar. Even though it has more nutrients, it should still be regarded as a treat rather than a staple.

CULTURE – Just like humans have specific groups of people bound together by culture, so do bacteria. A culture is a specific group of bacteria with attributes that support their continued growth. These are used during fermentation to create a whole lot of beneficial products like kimchi, sauerkraut, kefir and sourdough. High Mood Food is highly cultured!

KRAUT – A zesty, probiotic-rich fermented food known to reduce inflammation and build good gut health. Traditionally eaten as sauerkraut to provide vital vitamins over the winter months, it saved many sailors from scurvy due to a lack of vitamins. James Cook was the first to try in 1768!

LABNEH – This Middle Eastern delicacy also goes by the names of white cheese, yoghurt cheese or strained yoghurt. It's creamy and delicious as well as an excellent source of protein, beneficial fats, vitamins and minerals.

LOW CARB – A low carb diet is often chosen for weight loss, as an intervention or as a preventative measure against health conditions like Type 2 diabetes or metabolic syndrome. A low carb diet focuses on proteins, non-starchy vegetables and generally limits sweets, legumes, starchy vegetables and tubers as well as grains and grain-based products like breads, pasta, cake, cookies etc. Dodging hidden carbs can be challenging – they are often found in processed foods – so look out for sneaky additions to sauces and processed foods.

LUCUMA – If you imagine a superfood tasting like maple or custard, this is it. It adds a sweet rich taste to smoothies, desserts and ice-cream. The Peruvian fruit contains beta carotene, iron, zinc, vitamin B3, calcium and protein. Called the 'gold of the Incas' (because they used to trade with it) and viewed as a symbol of fertility and creation, lucuma is a superfood to look out for.

MACA –Sustained and lasting energy without stressing the adrenals is one of maca's claims to fame. It is also cited as enhancing fertility and improving hormone balance. The plant grows high in the mountains of Peru and the superfood maca that we know is taken from the root. It's also known as nature's aphrodisiac.

MATCHA - Matcha is a powdered version of green tea that originates from Japan, where it is known as the elixir of the immortals. It is lauded as a mood-enhancing, antioxidant powerhouse and also as a natural weight loss aid, pH balancer and detox agent. It comes from the whole leaf of the green tea plant and delivers 100% of the nutrients from the leaf. It is said to have about 137 times more antioxidants than regularly brewed green tea. Our Matcha Latte combines this power with almond milk.

MAPLE SYRUP – The syrupy sap from the maple tree contains important minerals such as manganese and zinc. It is a more natural sweetener that tastes smooth and silky with a caramel or toffee undertone. The quality is all in the grade. Use the finest, purest version when you feel like adding a bit of sweetness to your food.

MICROBIOME – The microbiome is made up of bacteria, as well as fungi, viruses and other microbial material that live on our skin and inside of us, in the gut and the vagina. We contain trillions of microbes and have many more microbial DNA than human DNA. The various colonies of microbes living in our digestive tract and bodies make up an 'eco-system' that interacts and evolves. The gut microbiome is the densest of our microbiomes, with trillions of bacteria living in our gut alone. Because it is such a strong and densely populated microbial community, it is important to our health and affects many areas of the body beyond just our gut. It has responsibilities in food digestion, immune regulation and mental health (90% of serotonin is created in the gut). Imbalances in the gut microbiome have been connected to varying conditions from Irritable Bowel Syndrome (IBS), to obesity and autism.

The microbes unique to your body are determined by what you're exposed to: where you live, your health, lifestyle, stress levels, diet, age, gender, your ancestors, who you live with, which dogs or cats you have and everything you touch can all affect the composition of your microbiota and impact your health and general wellbeing.

NUT BUTTER – Any nuts can be made into a nut butter by blending or grinding. Nuts are filled with fibre and protein and deliver sustained nutrition and energy. Make your own nut butter or buy a brand free from additives. Activating the nuts first and then grinding them makes it easier for the body to absorb both the nutrients and the healthy oils.

ORGANIC – The general understanding of this term is no added chemicals or pesticides, well-nourished soils for grown produce and hormone-free as well as chemical- and toxin-free animal feed for reared produce. Organic certification is awarded to food producers by associations that specialise in compliance auditing. It's designed to be better for the consumer and the environment with its natural ecosystems and waterways. However, many small producers cannot afford the costly certification process but offer the same and sometimes better quality of produce. We support local farmers and encourage you to look beyond the certification.

PALEO – This way of eating is based on the food that we assume was available to Paleolithic humans. It also goes by the 'caveman' or 'Stone Age diet' and typically includes vegetables, fruits, nuts, roots, meat, organs, fish and even insects. It excludes items such as dairy, grains, sugar, alcohol, coffee and anything processed. It has a few different interpretations, but in general favours natural wholefoods.

PREBIOTIC - Prebiotics can be seen as the fertilisers for good bacteria. They encourage the growth of good bacteria in the gut and bulk up your stool for easy and regular passing. Plant fibre from fruits and vegetables contain oligosaccharides which does not get digested itself but serves as food for the healthy gut bacteria. Prebiotics are found in the fibre of all plants. Some fruit and veg are particularly high in prebiotics, such as onions, garlic, bananas, asparagus, leeks, artichokes and Jerusalem artichokes.

PROBIOTIC - Probiotics are live micro-organisms that support your own healthy gut bacteria. The most well-known probiotics are Lactobacillus acidophilus, Bifidobacterium longum and Bifidobacterium bifidum. These beneficial bacteria or 'friendly micro-organisms' in the digestive tract affect our immune responses, our cognitive function, resilience and general mood levels. Our 5 K - fermented foods including kraut, kimchi, kefir and kombucha - all contain healthy bacteria. When you buy fermented products in the shop, look out for unpasteurised products as the heat in the pasteurisation process kills the good bacteria.

RAW CACAO – There are many reasons to eat chocolate! Antioxidants, omegas and vitamins are all present in the cacao bean. It contains tryptophan which causes elevated mood levels and is the highest wholefood source of magnesium, a mineral that's deficient in most modern diets. Magnesium relaxes muscles, the heart and the cardiovascular system.

The bean has a rich bitter taste but is heavenly when mixed with healthy sweeteners in smoothies or desserts. Look out for chocolate made with the true bean, or have raw cacao in a smoothie or dessert. Cocoa powder is a processed form of the roasted bean. High Tip: look out for 'cacao ceremonies' combining the goodness of pure 100% cacao with meditation and yoga!

REAL – One of our firm intentions is to offer 'real' food, which hasn't been highly processed or tampered with in any artificial way. It should not have been compromised by cost saving production methods and not have been genetically modified or artificially preserved. You can follow all our recipes without having to look out for harmful ingredients.

ROOIBOS – Rooibos or 'red bush' tea is grown in Southern Africa and has low tannins and no caffeine, yet the flavour is compelling and comforting alongside its far-ranging health benefits. It is rich in minerals and antioxidant polyphenols. Rooibos is known to be soothing, to relieve headaches and possibly supports fighting cancer. Growers consider the herb as an anti-ageing wonder tonic. It is even suitable for babies.

SEASONAL – Foods in season are fresher and by nature at their nutritional peak. They most often have benefits suited to the seasons. Winter veggies like roots and cabbage are suited to warming soups and stews. Colourful summer fruits are energising, with carotenoids that protect against the sun's rays. Eating locally and seasonally means that the produce hasn't been stored or transported long distances and it is therefore more likely to be environmentally friendly.

SCOBY – A SCOBY is a Symbiotic Culture of Bacteria and Yeast. It is the culture that makes kombucha from tea and sugar. It comes in the form of a gelatinous mass, which feeds on the sugar and yields a healthy, refreshing, slightly fizzy drink including lots of gut-friendly bacteria.

SOURDOUGH – Sourdough starters contain naturally occurring lactobacilli and yeast that ferments the dough for a sourdough bread. The gluten gets converted and is easier to digest. Eating bread made from sourdough triggers a more moderate glucose response than consuming normal bread. Many people who feel bloated on non-fermented bread feel great eating sourdough. Check out our chapter on how to make sourdough, and the recipe on page 63.

STEVIA – Used as a healthy sweetener, with a liquorice-like flavour, stevia is made from the leaf of a plant and contains no calories. Stevia enhances certain flavours and does not match with some specific taste profiles. However, it is brilliant as a sweetener because it does not cause any blood sugar spikes. It can be used in hot beverages, yoghurts and smoothies. You can use it in baking when the volume of the sweetener is not required: for example, you could use it in a cheesecake, but it is not suitable for a sponge cake.

WHEATGRASS – Famous for its detoxifying effect, one tot of juiced organic wheatgrass is likened to consuming the nutrients found in pounds of vegetables. Expect floods of therapeutic doses of vitamins, minerals, antioxidants, enzymes and phytonutrients in this blood and liver cleanser.

WHOLEFOOD – These are foods in their natural, original form, unprocessed and unrefined, without chemicals or alteration. The belief is that foods like fruit, vegetables, grains, beans and even milk and meat contain everything we need for digestion and absorption in their pure form without interference or additives. We use wholefoods in their natural form or we activate, ferment and soak them for easier digestion.

INDEX

Braised beef & onions 280

Braised black rice with fennel & chive 282

Roasted carrots, fermented gooseberries & wild mushrooms 137

Roasted jerusalem artichoke with kale & ACV dressing 258

Celeriac & apple slaw 282

Celeriac & apple kombucha remoulade 180

ASPARAGUS

Minted asparagus with fresh peas, kefir & curds 221

Poached asparagus in elderflower kombucha 232

AUBERGINE

Five grain, five herb miso porridge 93

Szechuan aubergine with miso & apple cider vinegar 149

Grilled aubergine 251

AVOCADO

Keto breakfast 103

Avo Smash 108

Jalapeno & avocado hummus 147

B

BEANS

Three beans & kimchi dressing 131

Kale & butter bean salad 149

Spanish chicken 169

Fermented radishes with edamame & coriander 239

Buttered runner beans & girolles with activated hazelnuts 245

BEE POLLEN

Immunity boost shot 68

Goat's cheese with bee pollen & roasted muscat grapes 171

BEEF

Bone broth 118

Braised beef & onions 280

BEETROOT

Beetroot shot 28

5k shot 69

Kvass 71

Beetroot, kefir & fresh curd 133

Beetroot, sesame & labneh hummus 147

Baby leaf & basil salad with fermented tomatoes 245

Red cabbage & blackberries with fermented beets 257

Beetroot on good gut croutons 300

BERRIES

Fermented gooseberries 137

BIOTIC MAYO

Kalibos and rainbow radish slaw 140

Devilled eggs 299

BLACKBERRIES

Fruit compote 86

Red cabbage & blackberries with fermented beets 257

BLUEBERRIES

Fruit compote 86

BREAM

Bream fillet 247

BROTH

Mushroom broth 117

Beef bone broth 118

Chicken bone broth 119

BUCKWHEAT

Ancient grain porridge 91

Five grain, five herb miso porridge 93

Good gut bread 107

Bone broth 118

Nutty spiced quinoa & buckwheat 134

Banana bread 199

Buckwheat couscous with apple cider vinegar & parsley dressing 267

Crackers for curry kraut & kefir sour cream 301

C

CABBAGES

Christmas kraut 52

Classic kraut 53

Curried kraut 53

High kimchi 56

Green kimchi 59

Carrot hispi cabbage slaw with shio koji mayo 140

Kalibos and rainbow radish slaw 140

Charred hispi cabbage with kimchi glaze 239

Red cabbage & blackberries with fermented beets 257

CARROTS

Baby carrots with smoked almond & kale crumb 139

Carrot hispi cabbage slaw with shio koji mayo 140

Carrot cake cookies 193

Buttered carrots with their tops & chervil 232

Roasted baby carrots with smoked almond & kale crumb 259

CAULIFLOWER

Curry roasted cauliflower 128

Ayurvedic cauliflower
rice 129
Miso roasted
cauliflower 129
Saddle of easter lamb with
wild garlic, caper berries,
cauliflower puree &
miso broth 225
Cauliflower bites 306

CAVOLO NERO
Roasted pumpkin, cavolo
nero & hazelnuts 283
Baba ganoush with Cavolo
nero Crisps 305

CELERIAC
Celery and cucumber
shot 68
Celeriac & horseradish
soup 125
Celeriac & apple kombucha
remoulade 180
Celeriac & apple slaw 282

COCOA NIBS & POWDER
High's chocolate
brownie 191
Activated trail mix 209
Spiced orange & cocoa
energy balls 207

COCONUT CHIPS & FLAKES
Paleo granola 95
High's 'Bounty' bar 203

COCONUT FLOUR
Chocolate chip cookies 203

COCONUT MILK
Tom Yum 117
Dahl 121
Ayurvedic cauliflower
rice 129
High's 'Bounty' bar 203
Coconut vanilla ice
cream 211

COCONUT WATER
Immunity boost shot 68
ACV Lemonade 81

COCONUT YOGHURT
Chia pudding 87
Ancient grain porridge 91
Dahl 121
Beetroot, sesame & labneh
hummus 147
Chicken with coconut &
lemon 167

COFFEE
Coffee kombucha glazed
parsnips 275
Bullet coffee 79

CORN
Charred corn with piquillo
peppers & kimchi salt 157

COURGETTE
Stuffed courgette flowers
with almonds, kale &
mushrooms 235
Seared courgettes with
lemon and mint yoghurt 249

CUCUMBER
Celery & cucumber shot 68
High-dration 81
Grillled romaine lettuce with
cucumber, mint & yoghurt 249

CULTURED BUTTER
Kefir cultured butter 33
Good gut bread 107
Cultured toastie 111

CHESTNUT FLOUR
High's chocolate
brownie 191
Almond butter cookies 197

CHIA SEEDS
Slow & steady seeds 90
Paleo granola 95

Carrot cake cookies 193
Crackers for curry kraut &
kefir sour cream 301

CHICKEN
Chicken bone broth 119
Pumpkin soup 122
Chicken with coconut &
lemon 167
Chicken with salsa
verde 167
Cultured coronation
chicken 168
Spanish chicken 169
Roasted chicken with lemon
& thyme 243
Cajun chicken skewers 303

CHICKPEAS
Three beans and kimchi
dressing 131
Jalapeno & avocado
hummus 147
Pumpkin & cumin seed
hummus 147
Beetroot, sesame & labneh
hummus 147
Tomato chickpea salad 148

CHICORY
Red chicory & fig salad with
fresh goat's cheese &
walnut 142
San Marzano tomato &
chicory with fermented cherry
tomatoes 233
Charred chicory with
hazelnuts & lemon 258

CHILLI
Keto breakfast 103
Shakshuka 105
Tom Yum 117
Pumpkin soup 122
Cultured coronation
chicken 168
Spanish chicken 169
Living hot sauce 176

Five alarm chilli 177
Spicy brown rice 244
Seared courgettes with lemon & mint yoghurt 249
Tempeh 253
Grilled prawns 277
Cajun chicken skewers 303
Tempeh spoons or skewers 309

CHOCOLATE, DARK
Low carb brownie 189
High's chocolate brownie 191
Chocolate chip cookies 203
Almond butter cookies 197
Orange kombucha chocolate cake 201
High's 'Bounty' bar 203
Activated trail mix 209

D

DATES
Almond butter cookies 197
Spiced orange & cocoa energy balls 207

DUCK
Roasted duck breast 261

DUKKAH
Turkish eggs 101
Dahl 121
Devilled eggs 299
Tempeh spoons or skewers 309

E

EGGS
Boiled eggs 98
Scrambled eggs 98
Poached eggs 99
Omelette 99
Shakshuka 105
Almost caesar salad 130
Biotic Mayo 178

Banana bread 199
Devilled eggs 299
Tempeh spoons or skewers 309

ESPRESSO
Bullet coffee 79

F

FERMENTED
Chilli sauce 177
Hot sauce 176
Red onion 229
Tomato 245
Gooseberries 137
Beetroot 257
Mushrooms 300
Radishes 239

FLAX SEEDS
Slow & steady seeds 90
Good gut bread 107
Baked green tempeh falafel 163
Activated tamari seeds 182
Carrot cake cookies 193
Omega fix seed bar 205
Spiced orange & cocoa energy balls 207
Crackers for curry kraut & kefir sour cream 301

G

GEM LETTUCE
Simple grilled gem lettuce 142
Charred baby gem lettuce with sunflower seed crumb 221

GOAT'S CHEESE
Red chicory & fig salad with fresh goat's cheese & walnut 142
Goat's cheese with bee pollen & roasted muscat grapes 171

Baby leaf & basil salad with fermented tomatoes 245

GOAT'S DAIRY
Minted asparagus with fresh peas, kefir & curds 221
Piquillo peppers with goat's curd & kefir 259

GREEK YOGHURT
Turkish eggs 101
Almost caesar salad 130
Seared courgette with feta and kefir 152
Grillled romaine lettuce with cucumber, mint & yoghurt 249
Seared courgettes with lemon & mint yoghurt 249

GURNARD
Chargrilled gurnard with capers & preserved lemons 231

H

HEMP HEART & SEEDS
Turkish eggs 101
Keto breakfast 103
Avo Smash 108
Omega fix seed bar 205

HONEY
Immunity boost 73
ACV Lemonade 81
Bircher muesli 89
Ancient grain porridge 91
Good gut bread 107
Red chicory & fig salad with fresh goat's cheese & walnut 142
Celeriac & apple kombucha remoulade 180
High's chocolate brownie 191

HUMMUS
Jalapeno & avocado hummus 147
Pumpkin & cumin seed hummus 147

Beetroot, sesame & labneh hummus 147

Saddle of easter lamb with wild garlic, caper berries, cauliflower puree & miso broth 225

Miso glazed king oyster mushrooms 269

Shirataki noodles with miso & winter radish 275

Beetroot on good gut croutons 300

Tempeh spoons or skewers 309

Herb crusted cashew 'cheese' balls 310

MUSHROOM

Mushroom broth 117

Buttered runner beans & girolles with activated hazelnuts 245

Miso glazed king oyster mushrooms 269

Sprouted spelt porridge with wild mushrooms & chives 273

Fermented Mushrooms 300

O

OATS

Bircher muesli 89

Ancient grain porridge 91

Carrot cake cookies 193

P

PARSNIPS

Coffee kombucha glazed parsnips 275

PEAS

Minted asparagus with fresh peas, kefir & curds 221

PEPPERS

Grilled sweet peppers with toasted pine nuts & lemon 226

Piquillo peppers with goat's curd & kefir 259

POLENTA

Orange kombucha chocolate cake 201

PRAWN

Grilled prawns 277

PSYLLIUM HUSK

Good gut bread 107

Carrot cake cookies 193

PUMPKIN SEEDS

Slow & steady seeds 90

Good gut bread 107

Pumpkin & cumin seed hummus 147

Activated tamari seeds 182

Omega fix seed bar 205

Q

QUAIL EGG

Tempeh spoons or skewers 309

QUINOA

Ancient grain porridge 91

Five grain, five herb miso porridge 93

Nutty spiced quinoa & buckwheat 134

Black tea quinoa tabbouleh 135

British quinoa with wild garlic oil 229

Quinoa tabbouleh with pomegranate 241

R

RADISHES

High kimchi 56

Green kimchi 59

Beetroot, kefir & fresh curd 133

Carrot hispi cabbage slaw with shio koji mayo 140

Warm millet salad with fennel & orange 223

Fermented radishes with edamame & coriander 239

Shirataki noodles with miso & winter radish 275

RAINBOW CHARD

Kale & chard salad with kombucha dressing 226

RICE

Five grain, five herb miso porridge 93

Omega fix seed bar 205

Spicy brown rice 244

Braised black rice with fennel & chive 282

Wild red rice with parsley & fermented lemon zest 263

RICOTTA

Beetroot, kefir & fresh curd 133

ROMAINE LETTUCE

Almost caesar salad 130

Grillled romaine lettuce with cucumber, mint & yoghurt 249

Rooibos tea leaves or capsules

Apple cider cleanse 74

S

SALMON

Cured salmon 165

SALSIFY

Salsify, watercress and lemon 283

SCALLOPS

Pan seared scallops in lemon butter 285

SESAME SEEDS
Five grain, five herb miso porridge 93
Beetroot, sesame & labneh hummus 147
Tempeh satay 161
Activated dukkah 184
Omega fix seed bar 205
Crackers for curry kraut & kefir sour cream 301

SHIRATAKI NOODLES
Shirataki noodles with miso & winter radish 275

SORGHUM
Ancient grain porridge 91

SPELT
Five grain, five herb miso porridge 93
Sprouted spelt porridge with wild mushroom & chive 273

SPINACH
High-dration 81
Sweet potato saag aloo 148
Broccoli & cashew pesto salad 151
Baked green tempeh falafel 163

SQUASH, SUMMER
Seared courgette with feta and kefir 152
Seared courgettes with lemon and mint yoghurt 249

SQUASH, WINTER
Pumpkin soup 122
Pumpkin & cumin seed hummus 147
Buckwheat couscous with apple cider vinegar & parsley dressing 267
Roasted hokkaido squash with za'atar 267

Roasted pumpkin, cavolo nero & hazelnuts 283

STEVIA
Apple cider vinegar 175
Miso tahini dressing 178
Omega fix seed bar 205

SUNFLOWER SEEDS
Slow & steady seeds 90
Paleo granola 95
Good gut bread 107
Activated tamari seeds 182
Activated dukkah 184
Omega fix seed bar 205
Crackers for curry kraut & kefir sour cream 301

SWEET POTATO
Oven baked sweet potato 155

TAHINI
Nutty spiced quinoa & buckwheat 134
Classic hummus 146
Miso tahini dressing 178
Omega fix seed bar 205

TEFF
Ancient grain porridge 91

TEMPEH
Tempeh satay 161
Sticky miso tempeh 161
Baked green tempeh falafel 163
Tempeh 253
Tempeh Bourguignon 279
Tempeh spoons or skewers 309

TOMATOES
Shakshuka 105
Dahl 121
Tomato chickpea salad 148

Tomato, sumac, feta & pickled onion 155
Spanish chicken 169
San Marzano tomato & chicory with fermented cherry tomatoes 233
Baby leaf & basil salad with fermented tomatoes 245

TURMERIC
Curried kraut 53
Immunity boost shot 68
Turmeric latte mix 77
Ayurvedic cauliflower rice 129
Cauliflower bites 306

V

VEGAN CHEESE
Cultured toastie 111

W

WILD GARLIC
Saddle of easter lamb with wild garlic, caper berries, cauliflower puree & miso broth 225
British quinoa with wild garlic oil 229

ACKNOWLEDGMENTS

The inspiration for High Mood Food emerged in my travels from Germany to South Africa seeking a sustainable way to eat out for real health.

Thank you, James Kuiper, at Sexy Food in Cape Town, for sharing your knowledge and enthusiasm when we started out on this journey.

At the time, London's easy dining options did not offer much that focused on gut health or which had been rooted in the slow food movement. Natasha Corrett was kind to advise in those early days. While the concept of fermented foods is ancient, it was the team at High who brought it to life and who kept the energy going as we grew and developed our business.

I wish to thank everyone who has been a part of the High team and who has supported this journey from café to cookbook.

Thank you to my chefs, Ben, Toma, Evan, Gabriel and Gui for all the time and hard work you put into the kitchen and developing the recipes. Martin, for cleaning never ending pots and pans! Alina, for being there from the beginning and helping on all fronts from café management to creative design. Nusrat, for keeping the café running on track and for bringing your positive mindset to it everyday. Steph and the entire front-of-house team - Sophie, Maddie, Antonia, Tash, Georgie, Tom, Sim, Solrún, Jenny and Goda, for your service to our clients and for always walking the extra mile. You didn't just sell our food, you coached and advised, and cheered up so many people on a daily basis - including me!

I am particularly grateful for the collaborations with Activia and Danone who share our passion for live cultures and a happy gut.

Thank you to all the wonderful young vendors we met along the way. Momo Kombucha, Chalk Stream for local trout, Club Cultered for their tempeh, melt chocolates and Cru Coffee are all highly recommended for home deliveries.

Camilla, thank you for your creative design work on the book and the photography, and Ola and Ceena for creating more beautiful images.

Barbara, my dear friend and nutritional expert, for always keeping us honest and true to our ethos. You always did ten times more research on any claim. Lindsay, for being a sounding board along the way.

To my husband, David, for your consistent support and our children, Leah, Caspar, Kim and Benji, all of whom have contributed in their own ways from recipe testing and tasting to spending summer holidays working behind the counter in the café.

Lastly, so much gratitude and appreciation to all of our patrons who supported our mission, showed up and loved our food. We share these recipes with you so you can continue to enjoy gut healthy food and ferments in your own kitchens.

Written by: Ursel Barnes,
Barbara Herscovici, Lindsay Barnes
Recipes from the café re-worked for the cookbook:
Toma Ziukaite (www.foodwithtoma.com)
Nutritional expert: Barbara Herscovici
Design and photography:
Camilla Lovell (www.camillajlovell.com)
Second Photographers:
Ola Boruch (www.aleksandraboruch.com)
Ceena Labuschagne (@christina_anne_)
Edited: Katie Fisher, Meze Publishing
(www.mezepublishing.co.uk)
Contributors: Entire High Mood Food team
Printed in Great Britain by Bell & Bain Ltd, Glasgow

www.highmoodfood.com
@highmoodfood

Published by Meze Publishing Limited
Unit 1b, 2 Kelham Square
Sheffield S3 8SD
Web: www.mezepublishing.co.uk
Telephone: 0114 275 7709
Email: info@mezepublishing.co.uk

ENERGY · HIGHLY ENERGISING

BRAIN · HIGHLY FOCUSING

IMMUNE · HIGHLY STRENGTHENING

CALM · HIGHLY RELAXING

GUT · HLY URISHING